CH00594635

Jane Wilson

Weigh of Life
Finding the Balance

I

First published 2002 by: Jane Wilson
18 Langerstone Lane
Tattenhoe
Milton Keynes
Bucks
MK4 3BZ

Jane Wilson asserts the moral right to be identified as the author of this work.

Copyright © 2001 Jane Wilson

All rights reserved. No part of this publication may be reproduced, stored in a retrieval system, or transmitted in any form or by any means without the prior permission of the publisher, nor may be otherwise circulated in any form of binding or cover other than that in which it is published.

The techniques and advice described in this book are the opinions of Jane Wilson based on her experience. Jane Wilson and Weigh of Life Ltd expressly disclaim any responsibility for any liability, loss or risk, personal or otherwise, which is incurred as a consequence, directly or indirectly related to the use and application of this book.
It is further suggested that all participants seek advice from their Doctor before embarking on any exercise programme.

Printed in the United Kingdom by Arrowsmiths Ltd. Bristol.

A CIP catalogue record for this book is available from the British Library

ISBN: 0-9542024-0-6

Acknowledgements

My friends and family helped me to write this book and I will be forever grateful to them all.

Thank you Mum, for looking after my children so that I could work. Thank you Dad, for being your own secretary while Mum looked after the children.

Thank you Rosemary, for taking the photos and Alison and Mike for letting me use your houses to take them in.

Thank you Cathy, for painstakingly correcting all my mistakes and giving valuable advice.

Thank you Lewis and Jasmine for your patience every time I said, "in a minute baby, I'll just finish this bit."

Thank you Matt for loving me, supporting me and inspiring me every step of the way.

Contents

Introduction

Let me tell you why. Why I have been struggling so hard to find the time to write this book, between child number one being at pre school and child number two taking a nap, while the washing machine is going for it's second cycle and there is still dog hair on the carpet that I haven't yet found the time to vacuum up! I've struggled to find the time because I feel so strongly about the UK getting fatter and fatter, when year after year we are spending billions on the diet and 'healthy living' industry.

So, why are we getting fatter? Think about it for a minute. There are more 'low fat', healthy eating products in our supermarkets than ever before. There are more health clubs and gyms than ever before and never has our obsession with weight and body image been more prevalent. But still as a nation we continue to grow and get fatter and more depressed and tired and hungry as we exhaust ourselves with one diet after another in our quest for thinness. It is believed by experts that the number of people in the world that are starving is very similar to the number of people who are obese. Now that is a serious problem with food, don't you think?

I have written this book because I believe (or rather I know) that there is still such a lack of information out there that actually seems to reach the general public. Maybe it's not a lack of information; maybe it is so much information that we are simply confused or overwhelmed. I know this because nearly every single day, friends, family, colleagues and clients ask me, what I think about this diet or that diet. Calorie counting, fat counting, points, sins, cutting carbohydrates, liquid diets, food combining, special soups, fasting. The list goes on and on and as we continue to fail each time we bang our heads against this brick wall, our self esteem, motivation and self respect falls into a deep black hole.

I come from a dance background where body image was an important focus for me on a daily basis. I was already, at a young age, struggling to maintain a balanced mental attitude towards food. I then suffered the tragic loss of my best friend to cancer in my mid teens. Food, which had been my enemy, then became my comfort. I was obsessive about everything that went into my mouth, how many calories, how many grams of fat, and the percentage of fat. How many hours would I have to exercise to burn it off? Every label was read and read again, checked and double-checked. Written down, listed, calculated. My life was spinning out of control and for the next four years I suffered through eating disorders. Starving myself for weeks on end, bingeing for days on end, gaining back the loss and then purging and exercising excessively to compensate. In short I was messing up my body and messing up my mind.

My recovery came from the realisation that I could only repair my relationship with food by finding out why my eating behaviour was so erratic and bizarre. Why I felt like an out of control wreck, why I was so obsessed with what I was or wasn't eating. I needed a balanced approach and I needed to address, recognise and overcome all the reasons I ate other than to feed my physical hunger.

I started to eat. I stopped all the silly diets; I ate loads of food, high quality and in high quantities. No more cutting calories and making myself exhausted. No more cutting quantities and feeling as though I was starving myself half to death. I was able to stop bingeing because my body was no longer crying out, begging and pleading with me for high fat, energy giving, fat cell-growing foods. No more hunger, no more depression when I 'failed', no more deprivation and loads of energy. This felt good!

By this time I was working in the health and fitness industry. I studied hard for my exams and I spent the next seven years helping other people to realise their personal weight control goals. Meeting with them week after week, taking them to the supermarket, helping them achieve their goals. I began lecturing to groups with the aim of getting people to stop feeling guilty, depressed, out of control, hungry, negative and tired. I wanted to convince them to stop dieting and start eating. Yes, yes, yes! stop dieting and start eating! I wanted to shout it from the rooftops. Eating, but eating the right things and that means going back to the beginning. Forget the years of brainwashing by the media and the diet industry and learn how to eat healthily again. A balanced healthy diet, rich in all essential nutrients with the right balance of fats, carbohydrates and proteins. The foods that we need to survive.

Unfortunately that is a lot easier said than done these days. The government introduced nutrition labelling for us, but the food manufacturers and supermarkets quickly found ways to turn the new rules to their advantage. Manipulating and misrepresenting the figures, confusing us and making us believe that products are low fat when they are not. Even the world-wide known diet corporations do it.

Why don't they stop? Stop and tell us the truth. We still have to eat. We will still buy food. They will still make their money. So why are they trying to trick us and make it harder all the time? Well not any more, because when I've finished my mission as many people as I can reach will know how to figure out the truth.

Pause… Deep breath…

If you're still reading this after that little outburst, you might think I'm a little bit bitter about something. A little bit of an attitude perhaps. If I've known something is wrong with the food labelling for years, why wait until now? Why haven't I been this angry in the past?

I suppose it didn't bother me so much before. Too little time, too much life to lead, clients to see, children to look after, dog to walk etc. etc. So long as I knew how to figure out my fat intake and my clients understood and successfully lost weight and I got paid at the end of the month then perhaps it didn't really matter.
Well EYES OPEN! Of course it matters. If my clients were being consistently successful and feeling great, losing the guilt, depression, hunger, anxiety and deprivation along with their body fat, then so should the rest of the country.

So I wrote this book.

I wanted to include a virtual shopping chapter. Supermarket visits with clients are always the most rewarding, for them and me. We walk around looking at every single food label, laughing at the lies on the so called 'low fat' products and picking up some naturally low fat, fantastic products like butterkist toffee popcorn. Can you believe it?

So I wrote to the biggest supermarket giants in the UK. If I'm going to do a store layout with an aisle by aisle breakdown of products sold in each area, maybe they would like to endorse the book as a whole healthy eating concept for the store. Give the customers the back up support that they really need to address there lifestyle problems and weight issues, tell the public the truth and have the nation stampeding to their stores for the chance to buy genuinely low fat products with out the need to scrutinise every label.

Unfortunately, none of them were interested. Which is a shame. Yes it would cost them money to change their food labelling (quite a lot of money I suspect) but wouldn't it be worth it? Wouldn't at least 45% of the nation (that's how many of us are overweight apparently) want to shop in their stores, safe in the knowledge that everything that said it was low fat actually was! And that they really could eat healthily at last and lose weight and feel great and look fantastic. Who wouldn't want to shop there?

What are they hiding from? That is what I don't understand. There are tons of fantastic items that are naturally low in fat and are not being promoted as such. For example, in one supermarket there are two 'low fat' curry sauces, both are actually high in fat! Then in their standard range there is a Rogan Josh, a Madras, a Jalfrezi, a Red Pepper and a Makhani sauce all low in fat. So why not promote the ones that really are low in fat and standardise the others? It just doesn't make sense.

What it means is that if we are serious about losing weight and getting fitter and leaner, we have to spend hours in the supermarket trying to figure it all out for ourselves, because they certainly don't seem to want to make it easier for us. After all the longer we are in there the more money we spend.

The other three supermarket giants? Pretty much the same story. One even said that it would be too confusing for the public to change the way we label products. I beg your pardon. Too confusing? Are you saying that we are too stupid to figure it out? That we couldn't cope with the truth? Why does it have to be confusing? I am going to use this book to show you how to figure it out for yourself. Yes, you may find that a little confusing, but if they just wrote it on the label in the first place, there would be no confusion at all.

So, Here I am on a mission to set the record straight once and for all. We will beat them at their own game we will learn how to overcome their naughty little tricks and we will eat and we will lose weight and we will stop feeling deprived and frustrated and tired and hungry. I guess I've said that before but isn't that how you feel when you try diet after diet after diet?

Getting Ready

So let's get started. I've set the book up for you like a six-week course. It's not a diet. I know, I know, it seems like a diet, writing things down, reading labels, making goals and stuff. But I just want you to take six weeks out of your life to re-train your thoughts. Hey, start with this little game. I always do this when I'm lecturing to a group it's quite an eye opener. Don't turn the page to see what's expected of you or what might happen next. Just get yourself a pen and do it right now.

Write a list of twelve words right here on this page, that you associate with this one:

DIET

1.	2.
3.	4.
5.	6.
7.	8.
9.	10.
11.	12.

Take a look back at your list. What sort of words have you written? Positive, happy words? Can't wait to get started kind of words? If so, congratulations, you probably don't even need to follow the book beyond the first few chapters. However, if you are like 99.9% of the groups that I usually talk to, your list may look something like this:

HUNGER
DEPRIVATION
LETTUCE
TIRED
HASSLE
FRUSTRATION
NO GOING OUT
MISERABLE
COTTAGE CHEESE
CALORIES
RESTRICTION
MOOD SWINGS

Is it any wonder that we fail time and time again if this is how we feel at the mere sight of the word diet? It is hardly surprising that our attempts don't last beyond the first few days.

We've got to get real. Stop dieting. Stop buying the low fat foods just because they say they are low fat. Let's stop starving our bodies by cutting volume and calories, leaving us feeling angry and exhausted. Wise up. Learn which foods really are low in fat, including the treats. Learn how to eat out and stay in control. Learn how to overcome all the barriers that have previously made you give up. Learn how to set up your support system. It is all right here for you. You will eat, be happy and get active lean and healthy.

Six weeks. That is what I want you to commit to. That is how long the learning curve takes, working through week by week. Don't wait until you've got a clear six weeks without Christmas, birthdays or any other special events. The chances are that you are ready now. Otherwise you wouldn't have bought my book. The next few pages are about assessing your readiness and you may decide that now isn't exactly the right time for you. But go ahead read the book and when you are ready you will have all the tools in place. This is real life now. No more "I'll start on Monday". You don't want to avoid the fun things in life. You want to learn how to enjoy them and stay positive about your new lifestyle. Read ahead if you want to, but don't rush the process. Even if you are only a few pounds overweight, the chances are that you have been unhappy with the excess for quite some time. So take your time now. Do it once and never never go there again.

About You

A little questionnaire before we get started. Answer each question as honestly as you can.

1. Your weight at its highest

2. Your weight at its lowest

3. Approximately how many times have you tried to lose weight in the past?
   Never   1-5 times   6-10 times   more than 10 times

4. How many times have you successfully lost weight and then regained it?
   Never 1 2 3 4 more than 4

5. Were you overweight as a child?
   Yes   No

6. How would you describe your level of activity?
   Sedentary   Somewhat active   Active

7. Aside from your general activity, do you take specific exercise?
   Yes   No

8. Do you have a desk or car bound job?
   Yes   No

9. Do you have children?
   Yes   No

10. How motivated are you to succeed this time?
    Not motivated   Quite motivated   Very motivated

11. Whilst following a weight change programme do you usually feel deprived?

Yes   No

12. How often do you eat because of physical hunger?

Always   Sometimes   Never

13. You eat something that you hadn't planned, a 'slip'. Would you then continue to eat more for the rest of the day because "I've blown it now anyway"

Yes   No

14. Do you ever eat large amounts of food rapidly and feel afterwards that the eating incident was excessive and out of control.

Yes   No

15. Do you eat more when you have negative feelings such as boredom, stress, depression, anger, upset?

Yes   No

16. Do you have positive or negative feelings towards exercise?

Positive   Negative

This quick, honest self-assessment is designed to set you thinking about how ready you are to embark on a weight control or lifestyle change programme. The consequences of not being ready are huge. Many of us start a weight control programme feeling full of energy and enthusiasm, but without thinking through properly the many changes both emotional and practical that need to be made in order to achieve long term success. The results are usually a quick loss followed by an even quicker regain, leaving us with feelings of discouragement, anger, anxiety and self-condemnation for failing again. All of these feelings wear away the self-esteem leaving us feeling hopeless and negative. These feelings then increase self-doubt about the ability to be successful next time around.

Readiness is a changing condition. Think about how you are best motivated, What is motivating you at this very time to make a start? If you are not truly ready for the necessary changes, you should wait until you are better prepared to deal with them. This way you will avoid feelings of failure and self doubt and go in with an open mind, ready to deal with the problems that you are sure to encounter and then successfully overcome them.

Take a look back over the questionnaire now and figure out your problem areas. If you have tried to lose weight numerous times in the past you may already hold negative beliefs about your ability to succeed and have already experienced the feelings of self doubt, guilt and failure. But you are here now holding my book, and feeling motivated. Believing in your ability is vital. You must put your past efforts behind you. This is different, this is a lifestyle change. Be honest with yourself, learn about your body and do it just for you.

Think about why you are particularly motivated to start the programme now.

If it is just because it is after Christmas and you think (or somebody else thinks) that you should, that's not enough. It won't work unless you have clear-cut plans for how you want to look and feel in the future. Something that will keep you on track when the going gets tough.

I have included a page in this first chapter for you to write down your long-term goals. These might include how you want to look or feel for a special occasion, to improve your health and fitness, to wear a particular item of clothing, or to keep up with your children or your friends.

Now is a good time to write a list of benefits and sacrifices. Take a look at these examples:

Julie

Benefits
- Look better
- Stop boyfriend nagging

Sacrifices
- give up chocolate
- feel deprived and moody
- Can't go drinking with friends
- Feel embarrassed about having to diet
- Hot sweaty exercise

John

Benefits
- More energy
- Feel fitter

Sacrifices
- Less drinking with friends
- Constant effort

- Feel healthier
- Look better
- More confidence
- Wider choice of clothes

- Learning curve to change long
  term habits

You can see from these lists that Julie is in a very different frame of mind to John. Not only is her list of sacrifices longer than her list of benefits, but her choice of words is very negative. She should wait until she is in a more positive frame of mind before embarking on a lifestyle change programme to avoid re-enforcing her negative beliefs.

Have a go at making your own lists.

Benefits   **Sacrifices**

Now take a look back at question 13. This is a really common problem, which quickly leads to negative beliefs about your ability to stay in control. This is my little wheel that I use to try to keep things in perspective.

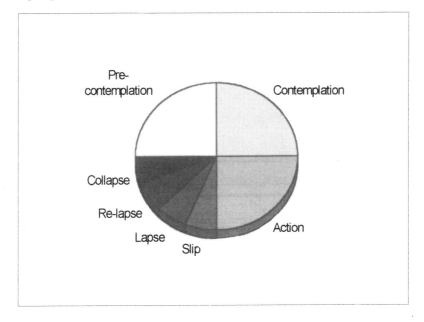

Read the wheel clockwise from the top left. No cutting edge research here you understand, just my personal way of dealing with that piece of fudge cake that 'fell' into my mouth. Pre-contemplation is the 'growing phase'! You are not thinking about your weight or your lifestyle. You are out there leading your life. Living it up, alcohol, takeaways, chocs, crisps, late nights, no exercise. Not that there is anything wrong with that occasionally you understand. But every day? Prepare to die! You are growing. Getting fatter and less fit with every passing mouthful. Then comes contemplation.

Something has made you feel that maybe its time to get in shape. You've moved on a phase. You make your plans and move into the action phase. That is where you are right now having bought my book, about to start the action phase. Then you have a king-size mars bar! A slip. Blown it now anyway, may as well have fish and chips tonight and start again tomorrow. A lapse. Tomorrow comes and your friend pops round with cream cakes to celebrate her promotion and you end up having a bottle of wine and a Chinese takeaway. A relapse. You go away for the weekend, indulge yourself silly and make promises to yourself to start again Monday. Collapse!

If you've experienced this kind of hamster wheel effect with your efforts in the past you will know that it's not easy to just jump straight back into the action phase and stay there. Something else will undoubtedly crop up to sabotage your efforts on Monday and you soon find that you are stuck for several more weeks back in the pre-contemplation phase.

You have to stop the 'on off on off' thing right now. No more diets remember. Let's go back to that king-size mars bar. A slip, that's all it is. So you had a mars bar. So what? Did you enjoy it? Good. Then don't feel guilty. Enjoy it for what it was and get straight back on your programme. The slip phase is an unplanned treat but you are so close on the wheel to the action phase that you can just slip right back into it, no real harm done. Remember that you have a life to lead. Don't sabotage your efforts on your guilt trip. Just stop there and get back on track.

The further around the wheel you go the harder it is to come out on top without negative feelings about your efforts. You will learn throughout the next six weeks how to modify your behaviour so that your programme is kept in perspective.

You will have to make some changes for sure and nobody really likes change. It is difficult and frustrating, you have to think about it, it takes you outside of your comfort zone and leaves you feeling bad when things don't go as well as you expect. But it's not all bad. You could relate that to anything in life. I went skiing this year and it felt much like a weight control programme. Difficult, humiliating, I wasn't good at it, my four-year-old son was better and I made a lot of mistakes. I didn't feel like I was improving as well as I would like, the progress seemed very slow, I got fed up and threw a few tantrums but I practised every day and I got better at it. I went through the initial learning curve and I started to see results. Then I actually started to enjoy it and now I want everybody else to do it too. Don't expect perfection from yourself. Change your thought process and you can do anything you like.

Getting Started

Right, here we go then. I'd like to start with a breakdown of the six steps to a successful programme. But hey let's cut to the chase. I know that unless I get back to the supermarket thing you are going to start flicking through the pages so I'll start by showing you how to overcome their misleading labels and start making some decent, well informed choices.

Reading food labels

To understand the labels you need to know a few basic nutritional facts and that is the framework for a healthy diet as set out by the government dietary guidelines.

- 55-60% of our total number of calories consumed should consist of carbohydrates. Bread, pasta, cereals, rice, potatoes, fruit and vegetables.
- 10-15% of our total number of calories consumed should be protein. Meat, fish, beans, pulses, dairy.
- 30% of our total number of calories should be from fat. An American College of Sports Medicine study showed that when fat is consumed, it is more readily stored as fat than if the subject had overeaten on protein and carbohydrates. The low thermic effect of fat (the energy needed to digest, absorb and transport fat), the ease with which fat is stored and the caloric density of high fat foods, make fat the obvious culprit in the development of obesity. Further studies have consistently shown that obese or overweight individuals have a tendency to consume a higher percentage of their overall calorie intake from fat than normal weight individuals.
  It is difficult to lower your fat intake to a dangerously low level so let's not waste any time stressing about that one! The lower the better!

Now we need to know how to work out the percentage of fat contained in our food don't we? Or why bother? If it says 'less than 5% fat' on the label then that must be great, right? Wrong. Lies? Let's take a look.

1 gram of carbohydrate contains 4 Kcal (calories)
1 gram of protein contains 4 Kcal
1 gram of fat contains 9 Kcal (don't forget that) Do you see that? More than twice the amount of calories (energy) than carbohydrates or protein. And just in case you were wondering...
1gram of alcohol contains 7 Kcal

Now that you know that there are 9 Kcal in 1 gram of fat, all you have to do is times the grams of fat in any product by 9 and that will tell you how many of the total calories are fat. Then divide the fat Kcal by the total kcal and this gives you the percentage of Kcal from fat (don't worry if your brain goes blaaah! Just bear with me on the technical bit for a minute). Remember we want to be looking for less than 30% of the total calories from fat.

Let's look at some examples

This first label is a mayonnaise made by a well-known and trusted diet company. Blazoned across the front it says 90% fat free. Check this out....
Per 100g
Kcals 125
Fat   9.2g

So we times the grams of fat by 9   9.2 x 9 = 82.8 fat cals
Divide that by total Kcal   82.8 ÷ 125 = 0.66

There you go. 66% of the calories (energy) obtained from fat! Did you see that? 66% fat? So the big label that says it is 90% fat free is a little misleading wouldn't you say?

There are laws to protect us from this kind of stuff of course but there are some easy loopholes. They get away with it because they calculate the percentage of fat by weight not the percentage of fat from calories. (Who cares how much it weighs)? For example, if it has 10 grams of fat per100 grams they can say it is 10% fat. Nothing wrong with that, it's true. But if the product contains 180 calories, that 10 grams of fat at 9 calories per gram, adds up to a whopping 90 calories and therefore 50% of what you have just put into your body. In order to have the true percentage of fat, you must always make the calculation by calories and not by weight. Calculating fat percentage by weight is completely useless to us. Look at it this way. It is said that the average women needs approximately 2000 calories a day in order to maintain her weight (more about that later). But you would never hear anybody say that the average woman needs to eat 2 Kilos of food per day, because it depends on what kind of food and how much energy it contains.

Next up a packet of 'lite' crisps. 33% less fat is what it says (less than what?)
Per bag

Kcals 130
Fat   5.9g

$5.9 \times 9 = 53.1$
$53.1 \div 130 = 0.40$

40% of the calories are pure fat! So they are hardly 'lite' are they?

'Healthy eating lower fat soft cheese' claims the label
per serving
Kcals 185
Fat   15.5g

$15.5 \times 9 = 139.5$
$139.5 \div 185 = 0.75$

75% fat. Is it any wonder that we are getting fatter and fatter if they can promote products like this to us under a healthy eating banner?

Now this is where things get really sneaky. Take a look at this supermarket's own brand of standard Tikka Masala Sauce and then their healthy reduced fat version of the same sauce.

Standard Tikka Masala sauce
Per 100g
Kcals 147
Fat   5.4g

5.4 x 9 = 48.6

48.6 ÷ 147 = 0.33   33% fat. Not great but now look at the low fat version

Healthy Choice Tikka Masala sauce

Kcals 92

Fat 4.8g

4.8 x 9 = 43.2

43.2 ÷ 92 = 0.469   nearly 47% So where is the sense in that? Apart from the fact that the low fat version is 28p more expensive is there any other reason that they might want to tell us that this one is better for us that the standard sauce?

Come on guys you shouldn't be trying to trick us like this. We've got you sussed and were not going to let you do it any more. Picture this, it's nine o'clock at night, you've just settled down to watch a movie and you feel a sweet snack attack coming on. You try to fight it by eating an apple (get real)! Then you remember the low fat individually wrapped (nasty tasting) little cakes that you brought just for this type of situation. Actually what you really want is a big fat chocolate cup cake that would definitely do the job. But hey, your will power is strong tonight and you're going to stick with your little low fat choc chip cake instead. Now hold your breath.....

Well known diet brand. Choc chip cake bar. It says 85% fat free on the label.

Per cake

Kcals 96
Fat   3.4g

$3.4 \times 9 = 30.6$

$30.6 \div 96 = 0.318$ Nearly 32% fat. Not horrific, but definitely not 85% fat free. Now remember that chocolate cup cake?

Lyons Chocolate Cup Cakes. No low fat claims here. We are talking their standard fantastic full fat gooey stuff that you normally wouldn't dream of eating if you want to lose weight.
Per cake
Kcals 125
Fat 1.9g

$1.9 \times 9 = 17.1$

$17.1 \div 125 = 0.13$ That's 13% Can you believe it? 13% That's 19% less fat than the low fat cake that you were conned into buying by a clever labelling and marketing department. Now can you see why I'm a little bit bitter, a little bit angry? They are selling you products labelled as low fat, which are higher in fat than the stuff you'd really like to eat. Not to mention more expensive, but don't even get me started on that one!

Now, enough reading. Go, go, go to the kitchen cupboards right now. Check the labels of everything in there.   Prepare to be surprised, maybe a little shocked and definitely a little angry.

Oven chips with less than 5% fat.

Kcals 163
Fat   5.4g

$5.4 \times 9 = 48.6$
$48.6 \div 163 = 0.298$ 29.8% fat. Now that 's not bad actually and I would say 'fine' if chips are what you want then these aren't a bad option at a fraction below 30% but still the lies. They are not, not, not less than 5%

I rang an Ice cream manufacturer the other day and asked them what 'non milk fat' means. Go check your freezer. Nearly all ice cream tubs have that printed on them somewhere. Big bold letters NON MILK FAT. Well, do you know what it means? It means that the fat in the ice cream isn't from milk. So what? I throw my hands up in despair. We don't care what's not in it. Just tell us what is in it for goodness sake. For what possible reason do they think we need to know what's not in it. Because it sounds good? Because it might just make people think that there is no fat in it? What? Tell me. I'm dying to know.

My message is clear I hope.
Never never buy anything again without checking the label.
Ignore anything that claims to be low, lower, light, diet, healthy or better until you've read the label and checked for yourself, because you can be sure as hell that it's certainly not always going to be the truth.

Now there is a bright side to this little story too. What about all the things that you previously wouldn't dream of eating if you were on a 'diet'? Check the labels.

Cup cakes

Fruit cakes

Parkin

Jaffa cakes

Scones

Ginger biscuits, garibaldi, fig rolls, café noir biscuits

Butterkist toffee popcorn

Twiglets

Pretzels

M&S crisps

Sara Lee apple Danish

Some brands of treacle tart

This list could go on and on and on. There are stacks of treats out there that aren't labelled as low fat but they are. You just need to hunt them down, now that you are armed with your new found fat formula.

Now I'm not suggesting you give up dieting and just sit back and gorge yourself on a variety of the examples I've just listed. But I am suggesting that you stop dieting, start eating a lower than 30% fat, healthy, loads-of-food diet which includes these naturally low fat, great tasting treats, to avoid feelings of deprivation. Get on with your life and start having fun and losing the weight.

Now, since I've ranted quite a bit, you may be a little confused about your new healthy eating habits so here's the breakdown:

The everyday basics of your diet should consist of:

Pasta	**Semi or Skimmed Milk**
Potatoes	**Low fat yoghurts**
Bread Products	**Fromage frais**
Rice	**Skimmed cheese**
Cereal	**Egg whites**

Chicken	**All Fruit and Veg***
Turkey	**All Herbs and Spices**
Fish	
Beans	
Pulses	

* Fruits packed in syrup and avocado should be limited.

These are the things that should form the basis of your diet. Make your meals as interesting and tasty as possible. You don't need to go to great lengths in order to do this. There are many low fat ready made sauces in the supermarket for you to take these simple ingredients and turn them into curries, chillies, creamy tomato pasta bakes, home-made pizzas (buy ready made base for convenience), risottos, stuffed baked potatoes, etc. etc. etc!!!

All you need to do is read the labels of the other foods that you are eating besides what is on your basics list. Now, you may still be a little confused about the fat formula and even if you're not, the thought of walking around the supermarket calculating every label will certainly seem daunting. But fear not. Here's my simple supermarket friendly way of shopping and label reading which will ensure that you stay below 30% without taking three hours to get around the store.

3 grams of fat per 100 Kcals

That's it. That's all you need to think about. If you allow yourself 3 grams of fat per 100 Kcals then you will stay below 30%. Let me show you how it works.

We know there's 9 Kcals in 1 gram of fat. And we know we need to stay less than 30%

3 grams of fat x 9 Kcal per gram = 27 fat Kcals
27 fat Kcals per 100 Kcals = 27%

Don't worry if you're still confused, just stick to 3g fat per 100 Kcals and you can't go wrong. If a product has 200 Kcals you are allowed 6g of fat. If it has 300 kcals you're allowed 9g of fat. If it has 50

Kcals you're allowed 1.5g of fat. Round up to the nearest 50 Kcals when you are reading a label and you have a very quick and easy way of finding desirable products.

I want you to remember that you are not going to diet ever again and I know that while you've been reading this you've been thinking, "yes ok, reduce the fat but what about the calories". Look at it like this, calories are energy right? So if you drastically reduce your energy, some diets recommend that you go as low as 1000 calories a day, is it any wonder that you feel tired and grouchy all of the time? Is it any wonder that after several days of starvation wild horses couldn't keep you away from the biscuit tin? Is it any wonder that when your body is trying to function on less than half the energy that it needs, you are exhausted and headachy and depressed?
What are you trying to do, starve yourself or lose the fat that is covering your body and making you miserable? If you are trying to live your life and function you need energy and if you are trying to lose the fat, stop putting the fat in. It makes sense doesn't it? Remember that there are more calories in 1 gram of fat than in a gram of carbohydrate and a gram of protein put together. You take care of the fat and let the calories take care of themselves. Think about this for a second... for the same amount of fat you could have three cheese sandwiches or one hundred bagels! Have I gone mad? Of course there are more calories in a hundred bagels. But could you eat more than two or three at one sitting? Not without feeling full and satisfied and energised and ready to carry on with your day, without having to think about food again for several hours. It works I promise. Eat lots, keep your metabolism high, feel healthy and

strong and lose that fat. I have included a lot more information about the damaging effects of reducing calories drastically on page 55.

Now, ready? Choose a day (today would be good) and lets get started with...

Week one

Here's a little six step plan to give you a taste of some of the topics that we will discuss in more detail in the coming weeks. Now you've got a grip on the food labelling we'll need to work a little on the lifestyle habits and behaviours that are keeping you overweight. Subtle changes are what you're going to make. Don't try and do everything at once. Use the book as your constant companion and diary over the next six weeks and take it slow and steady. If the thought of joining a gym leaves you cold, get round your mate's house and ask her to go for a walk with you. And don't force yourself to do anything that you don't want to.

Step One - Awareness

The first step in changing your eating habits is to become aware of them. After all, you can't achieve a certain goal if you don't know where you're starting from! Start to keep a food diary (only for a couple of weeks, otherwise we go back to diet mentality). Record everything you eat, including approximate portion sizes, time, whom you were with and how you were feeling. It may seem like a bother at first, but you will soon see its value. This little tool will show you many things that you weren't aware of:. Do you practically nibble away an entire meal while preparing it?

Do you half-consciously eat while watching T.V?

Do you eat too much at restaurants because you're 'paying for it anyway'?

Your food diary will show up these kinds of problem areas so that you can work on them in the coming weeks.

Step Two - Why do you eat?

Take a good look at your eating 'cues' – those things that immediately precede your eating. Do you eat whenever you are offered something?

Are many of your cues emotional ones?

Do you use eating as a means of quieting psychological pain? Making yourself feel better in the face of fear, anxiety, boredom, stress, loneliness or depression?

If you do, don't worry. It's not uncommon, but only by recognising these cues and by being able to differentiate between psychological and physiological hunger can you begin to make a change in the way you eat.

Try to feel the difference between external cues and real hunger. One big distinction is that psychological hunger is not satisfied by food! It is said that a successful dieter will respond only to that feeling of true physiological need for energy. Huh…I don't really believe that 100%. Everybody eats sometimes when they are not really hungry, but we will definitely look at how often and in what circumstances you might be doing this. For example, if you do it every evening while you watch T.V, you may have formed an unhealthy association that you will need to conquer. However if you have popcorn when you go to the movies even though you've just had a meal... hey, who doesn't? You're hardly an out of control freak! We will be looking at ways to overcome your personal cues throughout the programme and I will give you plenty of ideas that may help you along the way.

Step Three - Goals

The most important part of the programme. Listen. The most important part of the programme. **Do it and do it every single week for the next six weeks**. In my experience, people who set goals every week are always the most focused and therefore the most successful in sticking to their programme and kissing the fat goodbye. I have set aside page 38 to help you with some ideas of what your goals might be on a weekly basis and there is a page at the end of each week for you to write your goals on. But first, set some long-term goals. I have included page 37 for you to do this also.

Decide exactly how this programme is going to be successful for you and what you want to achieve, then write it down. Second, break your long-term goals down into smaller short-term goals; these are goals that you will set on a weekly basis to help you work towards your long-term goals. This will give you something to work for that is in sight. When you reach your short-term goal, reward yourself (without the use of food). You've accomplished something – a small victory – and should feel good about yourself. Take each short-term goal one at a time. Remember, it's a lot easier to climb a ladder one step at a time than to try to leap to the top.

Your goals must be SMART: Specific

Measurable

Achievable

Realistic

Time orientated

Always break your goals into their smallest form. For example:

- I will exercise three times this week
- I will exercise on Monday, Wednesday and Friday
- On Monday I will go for a brisk walk after work
- On Wednesday I will swim at lunchtime
- On Friday I will cycle after work

Always write your goals down so you don't 'drift' through the week. Know what you need to achieve each week and go for it. At the end of each chapter is a page entitled 'This Week's Tasks'. Your goals can be based around these tasks, or look through your food diary and see what you could improve on. Think about what is happening during the week ahead and make goals for any difficult situations such as visiting friends, meals out, birthdays or business lunches.

Step Four - Set up your support

If you want help, support and positive re-enforcement when you embark on a weight loss programme (and who doesn't?), you must ask for it! Tell your family and friends what you need and how they can help.   You'll probably be cooking differently and spending more time exercising. Your life will change and you'll need some support (like the friend that will take a walk with you every evening).   In the short term, don't be afraid to make changes in your life that will ensure your success. Be careful whom you choose as your support. Sometimes friends or your partner may actually try to sabotage your efforts to lose weight.   An explanation for this may be that your relationship with these people evolved with both you and them being a certain way, appearance and all.   Now your weight loss is a threat to the comfortable relationship, – because you want to change!

Step Five - Prepare and be nice to yourself!

Since you're now ready to get going on your weight loss programme, you're going to need some ammunition.   That is, you'll need to be prepared for the times when:

1)   Those external eating cues attack.

2)   You backslide a little (it happens to everyone).

First, have your healthy, low fat snacks handy when those externally cued urges to eat hit you. This could mean taking a cooler to work or keeping snacks in your briefcase or bag.

Second, keep in mind that your nutrition programme is a long-term decision, utilising moderation and an improvement in eating habits. With this perspective, an occasional slip does not mean the end of the world and total, humiliating failure. Because this is long term, it has to be realistic. You are not going to avoid restaurants and you are not going to never eat chocolate again. So you have to learn to modify. Try not to view restaurant situations as a problem, but rather something to be enjoyed. Don't always deny yourself the things that you enjoy most. If you want to have steak and chips, do so, but have a fruit based starter and skip dessert. If you are quite happy to have fish and salad then indulge in a dessert. Remember that what you do 90% of the time is what counts. 10% indulgence won't set you back and will help you to enjoy your new eating plan without the awful restriction and feelings of guilt and failure that many diets lead to.

Step Six – To weigh or not to weigh?

Most people use scales as a guide to success when following a weight loss programme. But how many times have you sabotaged any chance you may have of long lasting success by becoming a slave to the scales, allowing those numbers to dictate your moods, attitudes and food choices.

Who cares how much you weigh? Others do not see your weight stamped across your forehead; they see you and how you're looking and feeling. If you are feeling healthier and slimmer and firmer and stronger and fitter, then who cares how much you weigh?

I have seen happy, positive people who have told me they feel great and have had a successful week, suddenly feel bad about themselves, just because the scales don't say what they expect. The truth is that these numbers that we all make too much of can be very misleading. Bodyweight fluctuates rapidly according to many factors: hormones, water balance, training, time of day, time of your last meal, content of your last meal, exercise, the list goes on and on.

You should try to use your clothes, the mirror, a tape measure and the feel good factor to monitor your progress.

If you must use the scales, only weigh yourself once a week on the same day, first thing in the morning without clothes. Make sure that the scales are in the same place and are on a hard surface, not carpet. Lastly, if the scales don't say what you expect, shrug your shoulders, put them to one side and go and put on those trousers that are feeling looser already!

The most successful people are those that do not see their nutrition programme in black and white (as they're either 'on it' or 'off it'), but in shades of grey – sometimes a bit better, other times not so great. When they fall off, they get right back on and don't worry about it! The difference between a successful person and an unsuccessful person is that a successful person keeps going while the unsuccessful person gives up.

I like that. Cut it out and stick it on your fridge!

Long Term Goal Sheet

Name _____

Date _____

"I have enrolled on the 'Weigh Of Life' programme because I want to"....

1. _____

2. _____

3. _____

Assuming one of your goals is to lose weight, write three reasons why you wish to lose weight.

"I want to lose weight because......."

1. _____

2. _____

3. _____

Tips for making your short term goals

For the first couple of weeks you should make your goals based around the negative food behaviours that you know you already have.

Make sure that you are realistic and don't go for total denial, for example 'I will not eat any chocolate' (total humiliating failure is right around the corner if you go for this one).

You know that it is not realistic to deny yourself chocolate for the rest of your life, so think about your week rationally and decide on which days you will allow yourself a treat and on which days you will find it easier to go without.

Look at your diary and think about the times during the week that you know will be more difficult. For example, time when you don't have any plans and will be alone in the house, or a friend is coming over to visit, or an evening out.

Make a plan for these days, what you are likely to eat, maybe some extra exercise or things to do to keep you busy and out of the kitchen when you shouldn't be there.

Think about your work schedule for the coming week. Are there likely to be any unexpected lunch meetings where you won't be in control? Make a back up plan that you can follow the next day if you have an unexpected slip. Think about any situations that made it difficult for you last week. What will you do next time a similar situation arises? Build it into your short-term goals the next time it is likely to happen.

Make sure that you have everything you need available. Don't risk coming home from work to find the cupboards empty and a takeaway a very attractive option! Build your grocery shopping trip into your short-term goals. Decide on your exercise schedule for the week and write it in your diary. These are just some ideas to help you set your short term or weekly goals. It doesn't matter if you set similar goals each week or completely different ones. Just make sure they are realistic and don't try to change things too drastically all at once.

If you find yourself putting obstacles in the way, question your commitment to your programme. How serious are you about losing that fat? If you can't get out to exercise because you've got no one to look after the kids, stick them in a pushchair or on roller skates and take them with you, or go to the library and get an exercise video. I know you're tired by the end of the day but it will wake you up, increase your confidence, make you feel better about yourself, relieve stress and give you a feeling of well being and success. The same way it will if you resist that cream cake that you've been thinking about eating for the past hour. Don't keep thinking about it, throw it out! You need to be ruthless and selfish sometimes in your quest for success. But think about all the time that you give to your friends, family and colleagues. Isn't it time you were just a little selfish?

This Week's Goals

(Make at least one but not more than five)

➤ .

➤ .

➤ .

➤ .

➤ .

Notes…

Using the food diary

You should be as specific as you can when filling in the food diary (see page 44). The more information you put down the easier it is to see patterns emerging. If you are eating chocolate for example, you need to write down what was happening that made you want to eat it. "I was craving it" isn't much help. What was making you crave it? Did you just see an advert for chocolate? Is it just because you know it is in the house? Are you feeling stressed and thought it would make you feel better? Are you eating for comfort? Do you always crave chocolate at this time of the month? Until you have a clear understanding of your reasons for eating you cannot do anything to change them. Start keeping your diary straight away.

Here are some tips to help you.

1. **Time of day.** Always note the time of day that you are eating. If you do shift work or eat at strange hours for some reason, you may find it useful to note whether you consider what you are eating to be a meal or a snack.

2. **Food eaten.** Make sure that you write down everything that goes in your mouth.
    For example, 'a sandwich' is not specific enough. Write down how many slices of bread you had and exactly what was in the sandwich including any dressing, butter or spread.

3. **Portion size.** You do not need to weigh anything that you eat. It is not realistic to do so, as you won't keep this up in the long term. Note whether you consider it to be a small, medium or large portion. You should base your estimations on the recommended servings. For example if you buy a packet of fresh pasta that says it serves 2 people and you eat it yourself, it would be a large portion. If you shared it between two it would be a medium portion and if you had less than half the packet it would be a small portion. Most products tell you how many people they serve or give a recommended serving size.

4. **Hunger ratings.** The hunger rating uses a scale of 1-5. 1 means you are not hungry and 5 means that you are starving. You need to become very aware of your hunger ratings before you eat and should try to be around a 3-4. If you are eating when you are not hungry there should be some kind of explanation for this further along the page. We will be looking at hunger ratings further next week. This week you just need to be aware of them. People often ask me "How much should I be eating?" This is a very individual question, but you should eat enough so that you feel comfortably full when you have finished your meal. Remember we are going for high volume. Try this week just to concentrate of the content of your diet by reading the food labels and don't worry too much about quantity. Most people when following a weight loss programme restrict the size of their meals and this leads to hunger, starvation, and feelings of deprivation and ultimately bingeing when you can't stand it any longer!

I'll say it again: look after the fat and the calories will look after themselves.

5. **Where are you and who are you with?** Make a note of this to see if any patterns emerge. For example, do you eat more in company or do you eat more when you are on your own? Were you feeling any peer pressure? Do you eat more at home? Or when you are out?

6. **How are you feeling?** Make a note of your feelings at the time of eating. If it is a normal meal time, you may not notice anything significant, but this is particularly useful if you are snacking. Were you bored, upset, stressed, relaxed, happy, pressured, defiant, guilty etc?

Lastly, it is very useful if you write down in brackets or a different coloured pen, the things that you wanted to eat but decided not to in order to stick with your programme. Note how you were feeling at the time, what made you want to eat it and how you felt about not having it.

It is important to keep your food diary with you and fill it in throughout the day. Avoid leaving it until the end of the day or even the next day as little things are very easily forgotten.

You must complete the food diary this week. You will need it to complete a task at the beginning of week two!

Time of day	Food Eaten	Portion Size S, M, L	Hunger Rating 1-5	Where are you & Who are you with?	How are you feeling?	What else are you doing?

Time of day	Food Eaten	Portion Size S, M, L	Hunger Rating 1-5	Where are you & Who are you with?	How are you feeling?	What else are you doing?

Time of day	Food Eaten	Portion Size S, M, L	Hunger Rating 1-5	Where are you & Who are you with?	How are you feeling?	What else are you doing?

Time of day	Food Eaten	Portion Size S, M, L	Hunger Rating 1-5	Where are you & Who are you with?	How are you feeling?	What else are you doing?

Time of day	Food Eaten	Portion Size S, M, L	Hunger Rating 1-5	Where are you & Who are you with?	How are you feeling?	What else are you doing?

Time of day	Food Eaten	Portion Size S, M, L	Hunger Rating 1-5	Where are you & Who are you with?	How are you feeling?	What else are you doing?

Time of day	Food Eaten	Portion Size S, M, L	Hunger Rating 1-5	Where are you & Who are you with?	How are you feeling?	What else are you doing?

Week two

Here we go then. Hopefully you've completed all your tasks and at least seven days have passed. In some ways the first week is often the easiest as your motivation is high and you're committed to making the changes and completing the tasks that you set for yourself. You're also likely to have chosen a week that suits you with regard to the other demands in your life. But on the other hand, the first week can often be the hardest as this is when the changes that you make are the most noticeable. You may not have been fully prepared for how the changes affect you both physically and mentally, or something may have cropped up and challenged one of your goals, leaving you feeling frustrated. Whatever kind of week you've had, it was the start of your learning process and you can make this week's goals based around your first week's successes or challenges. Let's take a look at your food diary and your positive or negative feelings towards your efforts on each day.

- How many days did you feel were good days? _____ If you felt that all seven were good days, that's great, but read on, as the following questions may help you to think about your programme more objectively when you have a week that's not quite as easy going.

- List three words to describe how you felt at the end of a 'good' day

_____

_____

_____

- List three words to describe how you felt at the end of a 'bad' day

_____

_____

_____

- Now write down three positive things that you achieved on each 'bad' day.

_____

_____

_____

For example:

- Did you eat a nutritious breakfast
- Did you eat cake, but chose a low fat bun instead of a high fat pastry (have you been checking out the labels? I told you there were some delicious low fat options)!

- Did you have a takeaway but chose the lowest fat option on the menu
- Maybe you took some exercise
- Maybe you had three glasses of wine but normally would have had the whole bottle.

There will always be some positive aspects of the day if you look closely enough for them. If you feel there isn't anything positive about a day it may be that you will have learnt something from it about your behaviour and that will help you during your next difficult time. Remember that this is a learning curve and don't expect perfection from yourself. As long as you are thinking about your behaviour every time you 'slip', you are reducing the possibility of it happening again.

Lastly, look at your diary again and list three ways in which you could have improved each day.

_____

_____

_____

For example:

- Did you allow yourself to get too hungry at any stage?

- Did you plan each day so that you didn't have to buy high fat snacks on the run?
- Did you deal with any offers of food in an effective way?
- Did you have to deal with any emotional eating?

Based on your lists, write a plan of action for this week and include it in this week's short-term goals.

By the way, you will notice that I have put the words good and bad in inverted commas. This is because I don't believe in good and bad but rather choice and balance.

Now back to the dreaded question...

How Much Is Too Much?

Well, how can you possibly know? Short of sitting in a specially designed 'tank' at a research centre and having your every move and every breath monitored, it is impossible to know how much energy (or how many calories) an individual will burn in any one day.

Generally it is thought that the average women burns around 2000 calories a day and a man burns around 2500 calories a day. Having said that, I think the average women is thought to be someone who weighs about nine and a half stone, is 5 feet six inches and participates in light exercise three times weekly! Uuhh! So you see, as I said it's very difficult to tell! How many average women do you know?

The key is to recognise when you're hungry and eat, and recognise when you're full and stop eating (easier said than done).

But fear not, this week you are going to learn how changing some simple eating patterns can put you on the road to success.

First let's look at how your body may respond to your eating habits.

Energy Balance - The energy balance theory is based on calories in versus calories out. So, if you eat more than your body expends in energy, you gain weight and if you eat less than your body expends, you lose weight. There are 3500 calories is 1lb of fat.

However, there is another theory that completely contradicts this and that is the set point theory.

Set Point Theory - According to the set point theory, the body feels comfortable at a certain weight and strives to maintain this comfortable level of body fat, or set point.
When a person diets to drop below that level, the body thinks it is starving and lowers its metabolism (the rate at which you burn calories) in order to become more energy efficient.
There have been many studies over the years that have proved this theory to be true. Here is one example.

Research Study – Bray 1969 (Michigan University)
In this study, 6 obese subjects on a diet restricted to 450 calories per day for three and a half weeks, experienced only a 3% drop in body

weight, but a 17% drop in normal energy expenditure, including basal metabolic rate (this is the rate that your body burns calories just to maintain your most basic bodily functions). On the other hand, when normal weight college students ingested 2-3 times their normal intake of kilocalories over 3-5 months, they increased their weight by only 16 – 20 pounds, instead of the expected 75 pounds. The body attempted to maintain its set point by using calories less efficiently and increasing its energy expenditure. It also appears that a high fat diet increases the set point and that repeated bouts of dieting make the set point mechanism more efficient. In other words, it becomes harder to lose weight and easier to regain it. In light of this information, the challenge is to lower the set point. Fortunately, aerobic exercise appears to lower the body's set point by increasing the metabolic rate. Research has shown that after exercise, the metabolic rate remains elevated for hours, increasing the energy expenditure beyond the energy cost of the exercise itself.

Starvation

Every time you starve your body, it responds by panicking and preparing itself for the famine. This means that your body will lower its metabolism and store as much fat as it can when you do eat in order to survive. You may have experienced a diet before where you have reached a plateau and your weight remains stable even though you are still following the diet. This is a typical example of your body striving to maintain its levels of body fat and lowering your metabolism to meet the reduced energy intake.

So, what you must learn from this is to feed your body and maintain a balanced approach at all times. Lots of energy in, lots of energy out. Remember the 100 bagels?

If you have a day when you have eaten more than you would have liked, just get straight back on the programme the next day and make it a low fat, healthy, balanced day with perhaps a little extra exercise. Not a day of starvation in order to make up for the previous day's mistakes. This kind of behaviour leads to the binge-starve cycle which is not only a very ineffective way of losing weight but leads to feelings of failure, guilt and lack of control.

Should I eat earlier in the day and not in the evening before bed?
This is a question that I get asked very often and whilst it would seem sensible to eat more food during the day when you are at your most active and less in the evening when you are more sedentary, there has never been any scientific evidence to support this. It is generally believed that weight loss will occur if you incur a calorie deficit regardless of what time of day you actually consumed the calories.

Most people's lifestyles dictate that the main meal is taken in the evening. You may like to try eating more food at lunchtime and whilst still having your main meal in the evening, reducing the portion size. However in my experience I have found that most people still want to eat more in the evening when they are relaxed, making this method ineffective. Try it and see how you feel.

Eat little and often

Smaller, more frequent meals suggest that there may be less time for food to be stored as fat and your body can use all the nutrients in the meal more efficiently.

Eating also temporarily increases the metabolic rate whilst all bodily functions get underway in order to digest the meal – the more often you eat the more often you increase your metabolic rate!

Great news! But keep it in perspective. Smaller more frequent meals do not realistically fit into most peoples lifestyle and you could end up never being satisfied with the amount of food that you have eaten and therefore creating continual snacking, leading to excessive consumption.

However, sticking to three meals with some starchy or fruit snacks in between may be a better way of taking advantage of this theory.

Always eat breakfast

If you are not currently eating breakfast, this should be your most important goal over the coming weeks. The benefits are massive.

Breakfast is quite literally breaking the night time fast. It raises the metabolism and sets the body up for the rest of the day. Research suggests that the metabolic rate is increased enough to burn up to 300 Kcal by taking breakfast. It raises your blood sugar level and makes you less likely to snack on higher fat foods mid morning or lunchtime.

If you are not used to it and the very idea turns you off, start slowly. It doesn't have to be immediately that you get out of bed, but start to make a conscious effort to eat something as early in the day as possible and keep it light until you get used to it.

If you are not hungry in the morning, it is probably because you eat too much in the evening and also because you have trained your body not to expect food at that time of the day. This can easily be rectified as a new and very important part of your healthier lifestyle. Do it!

What About Sugar? (concentrate, here comes the science)

Sugar is a form of carbohydrate and therefore has the same amount of calories per gram as that of its more starchy counterparts such as rice and pasta.

However, its effect on the body is very different and therefore we need to keep in check not only how much we consume, but also when we consume it.

Your body needs to maintain 1g of sugar (glucose) per litre of blood all the time and it has two ways of obtaining the glucose that it needs to maintain its correct level:

1. The body can manufacture glucose at any time from reserve fats stored in the fatty tissue.
2. By eating starchy carbohydrates or simple sugars.

The body releases starchy carbohydrates into the blood stream very gradually and therefore raises the blood sugar to its correct level and maintains it there for several hours. When the blood sugar level starts to drop, you will naturally experience feelings of hunger again in order to stimulate you to eat more carbohydrates, thereby raising the blood sugar back to its correct level.

Simple carbohydrates (sugars) are released into the blood stream much more quickly and lead to a dramatic rise in blood sugar giving an immediate energy buzz. High blood sugar is dangerous and your body's defence mechanism is to stimulate the pancreas to secrete insulin into the blood stream. The job of the insulin is to chase the excess sugar out of the blood stream. However some recent research has shown that excessive doses of insulin secretion do not only chase sugar out of the blood stream, but chase fat out of the blood stream too, leading it to be abnormally stored. The fat travelling in your blood stream was on its way to the muscles to be used as energy!

Have you ever opened a packet of biscuits intending to have one or two and then proceeded to eat the whole packet? Were you aware of your behaviour and thinking 'why am I doing this'? But then carried on doing it anyway? Were you left afterwards with a feeling of complete lack of control and disgust with yourself?

This is the type of pattern that is established when you eat something high in sugar on an empty stomach. Your blood sugar level is low leading to feelings of hunger. You choose to eat a high sugar biscuit, which immediately gives you an energy lift and a high blood sugar level. A large dose of insulin is secreted, the blood sugar level is rapidly dropped, the fat from the biscuit is abnormally stored and you now have low blood sugar again leading to sugar craving and the next biscuit. The whole process is then continually repeated.

If you were to choose a starchy snack in response to the feelings of hunger such as a bagel, sandwich or slice of malt loaf for example, the complex carbohydrates would stabilise the blood sugar, which could then be followed by a biscuit without the negative effects of abnormally stored fats and further sugar cravings.

The conclusion of all this evidence is that you should avoid eating high sugar foods on an empty stomach. If you want to have an occasional high sugar treat, save it until after a starchy meal to avoid these negative effects.

And finally...
"I'm not sure whether I'm hungry or not"

Many of my clients have said this to me in the past. Trust me, if you're not sure, then you're not hungry. Besides, you probably weren't hungry when you were scoffing those two packets of crisps last week but it didn't stop you did it? Let's get real here, we all eat because it's lunch time, dinner time, tea time, movie time, munchies time. But how much of that time do you really need the food? Try not to be governed by the clock so much and re-adjust your patterns a little. Wait for your body to tell you it needs food as often as you can.

**Eliminate negative emotions:
that interfere with success,
(doubt, fear, guilt, anger),
leaving you free to concentrate
single-mindedly
on your important goals and
objectives.**

Everyone I have ever met that is trying to lose weight has negative emotions about their image or their ability to change their image. From my own personal experience I feel that it was precisely these negative emotions that were holding me back. Not believing in myself, spending too much time criticising myself, beating myself up emotionally when things didn't go quite as I'd planned, criticising myself in front of the mirror, refusing to accept compliments when they came my way.

At the time in my life when I came to this realisation, I was exercising excessively every day, 3,4, even 5 hours at a time, punishing myself in my quest for the perfect body. In reality I was unattractively thin, drawn, tired and depressed.

Positive attitude is a very difficult learned behaviour, you cannot just think 'ok, from now on I won't feel angry or guilty or miserable or doubtful anymore, I will always be positive and happy'. But it's a good start, it helps you to recognise your negative thoughts and start to turn them around. It helps you think about how long you have been unhappy for and whether what you are doing is actually going to help. The first time I saw this statement I stopped and thought, 'is all this exercise making me happy? Is it actually giving me the type of body that I want? Am I having fun?' You've probably guessed, the answer to all those questions was no. I was 20. My best friend had died three years earlier. I had been in emotional turmoil ever since. I was using food and exercise to try to hide and control my emotions and it had left me tired and unhappy with a very skinny, drawn, pale, stick like upper body resting on heavy, powerful dancer's legs. Totally out of proportion and time to change. That is when I decided to 'feel the fear, face everything and recover' (see mission statement chapter 3).

From now on every day you will look better than the last. Every day you will feel better than the last. You will stop putting yourself down, you will stay positive and you will, as the mission statement says, concentrate single-mindedly on feeling better and looking better!

You can do it and when you do, it will be worth it, I promise.

How to Reduce Fat Intake

I have listed here for you as many ways that I can think of that you can reduce the fat in your diet aside from reading food labels.

Limit your intake of added fats.
Butter, margarine, salad dressings and cooking oils have about 15 grams of fat per tablespoon. Use a low fat or a non-fat substitute instead. There are currently many reduced fat commercial products on the market. But always read the label.

Eat lean meats.
Substitute high fat cuts of meat for those lower in fats. Ask your butcher for advice if necessary. Try to avoid eating red meat more than once or twice per week.

Eat poultry instead of red meat.

Chicken and turkey usually have less fat than beef or pork. Poultry based luncheon meats and ground meat are also lower in fat than their beef and pork counterparts.

Trim and skin your meat.

Remove all visible fat and skin from meat and poultry prior to cooking.

Limit your portions of meat.

Limit your intake of meat and poultry by trying to have at least one or two days a week without any, substituting with vegetables. Try meals such as pasta with a spicy tomato sauce and eat fish on one or two days of the week.

Eat more fish.

Fish is lower in fat, especially saturated fat, than red meats and poultry. Eat water or brine packed tuna instead of oil packed.

Eat low fat dairy products.

Be 'healthy heart' selective when eating all dairy products. For example, use semi or skimmed milk, no fat or low fat yoghurt, and choose no fat frozen desserts instead of ice cream. If you eat cheese, choose a strong flavoured cheese and use it minimally. The lower fat cheeses are still high in fat and tend to have little taste, so you will be inclined to eat more of them.

Eat vegetable protein foods.
Dried beans, peas and lentils are both low in fat and high in protein and soluble fibre (which reduces blood cholesterol levels).

Limit your intake of nuts and seeds.
Although nuts and seeds have protein and fibre, both are high in fat. Beware the hidden seeds in granary breads.

Eat complex carbohydrates.
Replace foods high in fat with no or low fat starchy foods such as pasta, wholegrain bread, rice, vegetables, potatoes and cereals.

Eat fruits and vegetables.
Eat at least five to six servings a day of fruit and vegetables - both are high in essential vitamins, minerals and fibre.

Eat low fat breads and cereals.
Some breads (e.g. croissants) and cereals are high in fat (often saturated fat). Read the label and select low fat alternatives (e.g. bagels. I like bagels, I guess you've figured that out by now).

Limit your intake of fried foods.
Eat foods that have been baked, boiled, grilled, poached, steamed, microwaved or roasted instead of fried. Pre packaged foods that are coated in breadcrumbs have usually been pre- fried and the breadcrumbs are often stuck on using pork fat. Aaargh!

Use vegetable coating sprays.
Coat your non-stick pan with a vegetable spray instead of oil, butter or margarine. Or even better just soften onions, peppers and other veg in a little water instead of oil.

Use unsaturated fats for cooking.
Unsaturated fats (monounsaturated and polyunsaturated) are found primarily in vegetable oils (such as peanut, olive, sunflower and corn). Unsaturated fats have been found to reduce cholesterol levels in some individuals. However they are still 100% fat so use very sparingly.

Limit your intake of sauces and gravies.
Many sauces and gravies should be avoided because they are made with fat. Check the label and if it's not less than 30% use very sparingly.

Drain your mince.
When using minced meat, brown the meat and then drain off all fat before adding other ingredients.

Cool your casseroles and stews.
Make casseroles and stews in advance. Leave to cool so that all the fat rises to the top, then lift off the fat, reheat and serve.

This Week's Tasks

1. Keep a food diary for one more week. (included for you on page 69)

2. Make sure that you don't eat sugary foods on an empty stomach. If you need to snack, choose something starchy. If you are craving something sweet, choose something with a high starch content, such as an iced bun, fruit loaf or toasted muffin with jam or even cereals.

3. Look for three positive things that you have achieved everyday and write them down on the bottom of your food diary.

4. Ensure that you are eating enough and don't deny yourself food when you are physically hungry. Try to eliminate any non-hunger related foods that you may have recognised from your previous week's food diary.

5. Set three short term goals for this week based on:
    a) Exercise
    b) Difficult situations that are likely to arise in the coming week
    c) Any negative behaviour that you recognise from your analysis of last week's diary.

This Week's Goals

(Make at least one but not more than five)

> .

> .

> .

> .

> .

Notes...

Time of day	Food Eaten	Portion Size S, M, L	Hunger Rating 1-5	Where are you & Who are you with?	How are you feeling?	What else are you doing?

Time of day	Food Eaten	Portion Size S, M, L	Hunger Rating 1-5	Where are you & Who are you with?	How are you feeling?	What else are you doing?

Time of day	Food Eaten	Portion Size S, M, L	Hunger Rating 1-5	Where are you & Who are you with?	How are you feeling?	What else are you doing?

Time of day	Food Eaten	Portion Size S, M, L	Hunger Rating 1-5	Where are you & Who are you with?	How are you feeling?	What else are you doing?

Time of day	Food Eaten	Portion Size S, M, L	Hunger Rating 1-5	Where are you & Who are you with?	How are you feeling?	What else are you doing?

Time of day	Food Eaten	Portion Size S, M, L	Hunger Rating 1-5	Where are you & Who are you with?	How are you feeling?	What else are you doing?

Time of day	Food Eaten	Portion Size S, M, L	Hunger Rating 1-5	Where are you & Who are you with?	How are you feeling?	What else are you doing?

Week Three

Time to shine a light in your eyes! Answer (honestly) the following ten questions about the past two weeks.

1. Did you keep a fully detailed food and behaviour diary?
    Yes   No

2. Did you eat vegetables, fish or poultry instead of red meat at one or more meals every day?
    Yes   No

3. Did you limit your intake of fats to no more than two tablespoons in total of butter, margarine, mayonnaise or oil every day?
    Yes   No

4. Did you take some exercise that elevated your heart rate for 20 minutes or more on three or more days?
    Yes   No

5. Did you use low fat dairy products every day?
    Yes   No

6. Did you eat a nutritious breakfast every day?
    Yes   No

7. Did you choose starchy snacks instead of sugary snacks every day?
   Yes   No

8. Did you save any sugary treats to eat until after a starchy meal?
   Yes   No

9. Did you eat snacks at planned times only?
   Yes   No

10. Did you limit your alcoholic intake to no more than 1 per day or equivalent (e.g. none on Friday but two on Saturday?)
    Yes   No

Hopefully you answered yes to all ten questions. Don't worry if you didn't, but any questions answered no will show up the areas you need to continue to concentrate on in the coming weeks.

We are kind of leaving the food issues behind a little this week and are going to start to concentrate more on the psychological, emotional and social aspects of things.

Feel The Fear
Face Everything
And Recover

During my recovery from my eating disorder, I stuck this statement in a frame next to my bed. It was the first thing that I saw every morning and the last thing that I saw at night. For me, the statement was about putting the fear of food and the fear of failure behind me. Learning to face up to my fears and stop them from controlling me. Learning to escape the feeling that food was controlling me. I had to be in control. I had to be strong and I had to be focused and to do that I had to face everything head on and learn how to deal with any negative behaviour that was contributing to my problems. I recovered.

Whatever your fears, this statement will probably hold some meaning for you. Dieting treats the symptoms of over-eating. Face the reasons for your over-eating and recover forever.

Lets get started by....

Identifying Barriers

Barriers are things, people or events that have previously or are currently stopping you from achieving your goals. The next couple of pages will give you a whole stack of ideas that will help you to overcome some of the most common barriers. Not all of them will be relevant to you, but it is a good idea to get yourself a highlighter pen and mark off any ideas that you think may be useful. One of this week's tasks is to write yourself an intervention plan and you can use your highlighted ideas to start you off.

Think about the barriers that you have come up against in the past. Questions you might ask yourself should include:

1. Last time I tried to lose weight, what made me stop?

2. What made my last attempt unsuccessful?

3. What barriers do I regularly come up against that make it more difficult for me?

4. How do I propose to get over them this time?

5. What plans should I make?

Before continuing with the programme you must have a full understanding of your past failures to ensure success this time. Think carefully about all the things that have previously made you give up and how you will conquer those problems this time around. I have included a page for your intervention plan at the end of the chapter.

Here is your list of ideas:

1. Buy foods from a pre written list. Entering the supermarket is a dangerous game. You are suddenly surrounded by all sorts of tempting offers and smells. Make a list before you go. Enter, buy what's on your list and leave quickly.

2. Buy foods only after a full meal. Never go shopping when you are hungry, it is much more difficult to make rational choices.

3. Keep food in the kitchen only. Make your home a supportive environment by keeping food out of sight. Make sure that all food in the kitchen is in the cupboards; if you keep a biscuit tin on the worktop you will be tempted by them every time you walk into the kitchen.

4. Eat only in the dining room. Making some rules for yourself about appropriate places to eat may help you to reduce excessive snacking.

5. Do nothing else whilst eating. Try to enjoy your meal both mentally and physically. If you are trying to do other tasks at the same time as eating, your brain often doesn't register that a meal has been eaten and so although your hunger may be satisfied your appetite is not, leading to over-eating.

6. Clear dishes and leftovers immediately. Do not run the risk of returning to the kitchen later to clear up and eating the left over dessert!

7. Eat in company. Eating with someone who knows about your programme will make it easier for you to exercise portion control.

8. Prepare and serve sufficient for one helping per person only. Make sure you know how much to cook and measure it first. If you cook too much, the chances are you will eat it anyway.

Social Barriers – The things that people say.

1. "Go on try some home-made cake, just one piece won't hurt". The best way to deal with these situations is to say "no thank you I'm not hungry". If you say that you're not hungry people don't usually say, "I think you should have it anyway" because it doesn't make sense. However, If they think that you want it but are trying to resist, they will generally try to pressure you.

2. "You're getting too thin". Unless you think that this is a possibility, the chances are that your friends are uncomfortable with the changes you have made and are feeling insecure about themselves. Don't let them subconsciously sabotage your efforts. If they have made this comment you are obviously doing well. Keep going until you reach your personal goals.

3. "Don't let good food go to waste" If you were raised with this attitude it is a very difficult one to break. You must remind yourself that it is far more of a waste to put it into your body than it is to put it into the bin.

Appetite Control

Our appetite is controlled by a hormone, which is stimulated when we start eating. A message is sent to the brain and then to the stomach as an appetite control mechanism that tells us we have eaten enough. However it can take up to twenty minutes for this process to happen during which time we have often already over-eaten.

Have you ever eaten a large meal and afterwards felt that you are so uncomfortably full that you have to undo your clothes? If you had felt like this whilst you were still eating you wouldn't have continued and this is a typical example of the time delay.

The answer is to slow down your eating so that the message gets through before you over-eat.

Some studies have shown that fat takes longer to stimulate the controlling hormone than protein or carbohydrate and so we are more likely to over-eat foods that are high in fat.

In one British experiment, a group of unknowing people were put in front of a buffet containing only high fat foods and asked to eat as much as they needed to feel comfortably full.

The following week, the same group of people were put in front of a buffet containing only low fat foods and again asked to eat as much as they needed to feel comfortably full.

The results were that this same group of people consumed almost double the amount of high fat food than they did of the low fat food, therefore indicating that it took longer for their appetites to be satisfied by the high fat food.

So… eat low fat food and take your time!

Barrier Situations

We've now covered common barriers, social barriers, speed of eating and content of the food, but what about emotional eating? Eating because you are bored, tired, upset or angry?

Think about how you tend to respond in these situations and why you may use food as a source of comfort.

Write a list of things that you might do to make yourself feel better next time you're feeling this way instead of eating.

It is important to hold onto conscious thoughts and feelings. Think about what sort of day you have when you've over-eaten. How do you feel? Guilty, angry, bad about yourself, failure etc? Try to think ahead as to how you might feel after the event, before you indulge.

Alternatively, how do you feel when your day has gone according to plan? Positive, healthy, slim, successful and in control! Remind yourself of this before you indulge.

Identifying Support

Lack of support becomes a barrier! You have to create an environment for success by recruiting and building a network of support. Think about who or what might help you achieve your goals and how you are best motivated.

What might help?

- Keep a food diary

- Set your goals and write them down.

- Set up a reward system and treat yourself every time you lose 5lbs

- Leave messages for yourself in the biscuit tin to remind you that you shouldn't be there!

- Find a picture of yourself at a time when you looked and felt good about yourself and put it in a frame by your bed. This will motivate you as you start the day.

- Find an item of clothing that you want to wear again but is slightly too tight and hang it up in a prominent place in the bedroom as a reminder of your goals.

- As you lose the weight, throw away everything that becomes too big for you. By doing this you are making a positive decision never to go back there again. Keeping hold of these old clothes shows a negative belief in yourself to maintain the new you and gives you a safety net that you can do without.

Who might help?

- Family

- Friends

- Partner

- Colleagues
-

Choose your support very carefully. The people you choose must positively encourage the changes that you are trying to make. It is no good having someone whose attitude is "oh, here we go again" Drag a friend out for yet another walk, ask another family member to go to the supermarket. There may be a group of colleagues or friends who may also want to lose weight. Constantly look for ways in which you can maintain your motivation.

Do you have a supportive environment?

- Re-organise your kitchen cupboards. If you keep the biscuits in the same cupboard as the tea and coffee they will tempt you every time you make a drink! If you have to have high fat snacks in the house for other members of the family, keep them in a separate cupboard. You will then only be confronted by them if you make a conscious decision to indulge yourself, rather than just because they happened to be there!

- Make sure that your time is accounted for so that you don't find yourself alone in the house with nothing to do but eat!

- Keep some low fat treats in a separate place for yourself, so that you've always got something to snack on if necessary.

- Keep all food away in the cupboards.

Although you could be your own support, using your own planning, self control and own positive reinforcement, most people need some help and encouragement along the way. However you do have to ask for it, whilst continually seeking your own source of self satisfaction.

Eating Out & On the Run

Everyone wants to enjoy social eating situations and you may have found these very negative experiences when trying to lose weight in the past. But since this is a lifestyle programme you cannot avoid eating out ever again and you will probably run into these situations quite early on in your programme. You can still enjoy these social events; they just take a little planning. Of course if you only eat out occasionally you may throw caution to the wind. Enjoy, eat whatever you like and make up for it the next day with an extra exercise session. But if you eat out regularly, you will need to use these following pages as a bible!

I have listed here some tips that may help you.

1. If you are eating out with friends, offer to organise and book the restaurant, that way you can choose a restaurant where you know you will be able to make a healthy choice from the menu.

2. If someone else has booked the restaurant and you are not familiar with it, call in ahead of time and take a look at the menu. Decide what you will eat when you get there and stick to it.

3. Don't drink alcohol before you have started to eat as you will incur a quick rise and fall in blood sugar level, leaving you feeling even hungrier and running the risk of your body abnormally storing fats from the meal. (Refer back to week two).

4. Decide before you go how much alcohol you will allow yourself and stick to it. Try to drink a glass of water for every alcoholic drink that you have to reduce the total number you consume. Obviously the best option is to drive so that you cannot drink at all.

5. Avoid eating the bread that is usually served in restaurants. Since you are about to eat a large meal, you certainly don't need it.

6. Avoid being starving when you arrive at the restaurant. A good tip is to delay the rest of the day's meals so that you are not so hungry. Maybe have breakfast at ten o'clock and lunch at three o'clock so that you can easily get through to seven or eight o'clock with out extra snacks or excessive hunger. (This is a top tip, try it!)

7. Ask for dressings to be served on the side so that you can control the amount.

8. Don't order side dishes until your meal arrives, it may be bigger than you think.

9. Most restaurants serve larger than average portions. Ask for a smaller portion or offer the extra to someone else at the table. "I'm paying for it so I may as well eat it" is an attitude that no longer fits into your lifestyle.

10. Don't be shy to ask how something is cooked or prepared, if you are not sure what's in it. Most waiters are knowledgeable about the food they are serving and do not mind sharing this information with you.

11. Don't be shy to ask the restaurant to cook or prepare something differently. Usually they will try to help you and if you are paying for it, you may as well try to get exactly what you want!

12. If it is a very special occasion and you want to forget your programme for the night, be sure to plan in advance and make the two days beforehand very low fat, cutting any extras that you may have been allowing yourself. Enjoy yourself and then get straight back on track the next day.

13. If you are invited to eat with friends let the hostess know of your programme. If you were having friends for dinner you would want them to enjoy themselves and the food. So, they too will be happy to accommodate you.

14. If you are invited to a dinner party where you will not know the hostess very well, avoid the bread, eat the first and main course but skip dessert by telling the hostess that the meal was so delicious and you couldn't possibly eat any more! Then relax and enjoy the rest of the evening knowing that you maintained control.

15. If you are going to a party where there is likely to be a buffet, you should eat a healthy low fat meal before you go and keep away from the buffet. If you are not hungry this shouldn't be too difficult. Most buffet foods and snacks are very high in fat.

16. If you do choose to eat the buffet, make your choices as sensible as possible, avoiding pastries, pies, sausages and sandwiches with high fat fillings. Take your plate to the buffet and fill it just

once so that you are aware of exactly how much you have eaten. Picking at the buffet can easily lead to over consumption as you lose track of how much you have had. Use the party atmosphere to dance and burn calories!

17. If you are planning to travel, you should always take food supplies with you. It is often difficult to get a healthy low fat snack at motorway services or airports, especially if you are travelling at odd times. Take a cooler with you.

18. If you are staying in a hotel, call ahead and ask the hotel for a room with a refrigerator so that you can keep some low fat snacks available.

There should not be any situation in which you cannot make wise choices. As long as you plan ahead, inquire and take control of the situation at every opportunity, you'll discover a new-found freedom in your successful nutrition programme.

Your Personal Intervention Plan

Make a list of:

- All your negative thoughts about your body image

- All your negative behaviours with regard to food

- All the things that you feel have contributed to your weight gain

- All the things that usually make you give up on a 'diet'

- All the things that you feel make it more difficult for you to achieve your goal.

Alongside your first set of lists, make a list of:

- Some positive thoughts about your new lifestyle and body image. Visualise your goal, how you will feel when you get there and what you would like to do.

- What you can do about your old negative behaviours to make sure they don't interfere with your new lifestyle.

- What changes you intend to make to deal with the barriers that have contributed to your weight gain.

- How you plan to overcome the things that made you give up on your last weight loss plan.

- How you can reduce or eliminate the things that are making it difficult for you to achieve your goals.

Use the ideas that you highlighted as you read through the previous pages to help you.

This task will take you quite some time and you may find it easier to make a start and then add to it over the coming weeks. Every time you find yourself in a difficult situation you should write it on your list and make a plan of action to deal with that situation next time it happens.

The following pages are left blank for you to write your plans and lists.

Don't skip this task as it is very important to the success of your programme.

My Intervention Plan

This Week's Tasks

1. Using the suggested lists on your personal intervention plan, start to make your list of past and current barriers. Alongside each one write down possible solutions that could help you overcome these barriers this time round.

2. Think about the speed at which you eat and how often you eat 'on the run' or whilst trying to do other tasks. Make some goals to try to reduce both this week and notice the difference.

3. Spend some time thinking about and then setting up your support system. Use the notes to help you. (Don't skip this task)

4. Re-organise your kitchen cupboards to make sure that the kitchen is a supportive environment.

5. Experiment with some attractive food presentation. For example, make a large fruit salad and dress with some low fat yoghurt or fromage frais rather than just put it in a fruit bowl. Or make a large platter of highly coloured raw baby vegetables such as: baby carrots, corn, radishes, cucumber, cherry tomatoes etc. and serve with a low fat dip.

6. At some point you must give up the food diary. Although it can be a useful tool, it is unrealistic to do it long term. Give it up this week if you feel ready. If you choose to continue with it, make sure that you use the notes in week two to analyse your

diary at the end of the week. There is no point to it, unless you look back and try to recognise the changes that need to be made.

All of this week's tasks will take quite a while to complete, they are all important to the success of your programme and my advice is not to continue on to the next chapter until you have completed them. You can also add to them later in the programme if you wish.

This Week's Goals

(Make at least one but not more than five)

➢ .

➢ .

➢ .

➢ .

➢ .

Notes...

Week Four

Gently does it…small print so as not to scare…This chapter is about exercise. Aaargh!

Wait! Please don't skip past this chapter, I promise I won't tell you all the usual stuff. Exercise is great, it's fun, it's good for you, it will make you feel better!? Etc etc. Well I couldn't resist just a little. But I want to put it into perspective for you. You're probably doing another little word association game in your mind right now… Pain, humiliation, exhaustion, torture. But it doesn't have to be like that. Read on (please).

Only 20% of health club members are regular users (at least once a week). 60% are occasional users (once in a blue moon)? and 20% of members pay a fortune month in, month out, yet never set foot inside the place. And why? O.K you're right, probably because of the pain, humiliation, exhaustion and torture. Because they tried to use all the high tech machines on their first visit. Because they had to leave the aerobics class in the first ten minutes after failing miserably to keep up. Because they got crushed by one of the beautiful people during the 'double grapevine twist' (what the hell is that all about)? Because the young stud of a fitness instructor insisted on squeezing their fat with what looked like pliers, in order to tell them their body fat percentage! Or because they were refused an exercise programme without a note from their doctor because they were so unfit!

Well, I've worked in the Health and Fitness industry for years and I would love to tell you that it's not at all like that. But I know that unfortunately for many, that is exactly what it's like. So if you aren't too confident about joining a club, then don't (well not yet anyway).

Exercise is only enjoyable if it is done within your fitness level and the reason some people hate it is because they try to work at somebody else's fitness level. The aerobics class for example, the pressure to keep up, the pre set gym programme, based on what the instructor that you've never met before, thinks you should do.

You have to start at your own pace and all you have to do is increase the amount of oxygen that you take in. That's it just a little more of the stuff that we all take for granted. Oxygen. How? By increasing your breathing rate. How? By simply walking to the end of the road if you like, or by playing with your children in the park, or by taking the stairs instead of the escalator. If you haven't exercised in years and you are overweight and you've been eating a high fat diet, your goal is to just start moving. Increasing your oxygen intake a little bit at a time and stick with it. You'll get fitter and stronger and leaner and more confident. Then walk into the gym, safe in the knowledge that you don't have to have a fitness assessment if you don't want to; you don't have to use all the machines; you don't have to keep up with the aerobic instructor. You can modify, work at your own pace and have fun.

I have used this chapter to explain the pros and cons of working too hard or not hard enough, staying within your fitness level and increasing your general day to day activity. I have included some strength exercises for you to do at home and some stretching exercises to increase your flexibility or just to help you to relax.

Activity levels

Last year, I was asked to write an article for a web site. They gave me this headline... '80% of losing weight is diet and 20% is exercise' This is a true statement, but how did we gain so much weight in the first place? Escalators, cars, power steering, doors open without us having to push them, central locking so that you don't even have to walk around your car! Washing machines, dishwashers, drive through fast food, remote controls. The list goes on and on. Think about how much money the nation spends on developing and advertising new high fat, high sugar, convenient, cheap foods and then how much money we spend on trying to lose the weight we've gained. It's crazy.

Place yourself back in primitive times for a moment. Man goes out to hunt for food, woman stays at home to care for the children and conserve energy. The next meal will be a large one, but then you may not eat again for days. You need to conserve your energy for as long as you can.

Fast-forward a few thousand years and you get all the labour saving devices you could ever hope for, as much food as you want to eat and as little activity as possible. But still we have people that love exercise and make it a regular part of their daily life and we have people that loathe exercise and avoid it if possible.

Here's my theory, again no cutting edge research here, and just my personal opinion. I think that some of us are still genetically influenced by our primitive relations and that some of us are designed to 'hunt' and some of us are designed to 'conserve energy'.

Are you exercise resistant?

Do you leave things at the bottom of the stairs to take up later?

Do you wait until someone else goes out to the kitchen and then ask them to put the kettle on rather than get up and do it yourself?

When you visit your local shopping centre, do you drive around for a while waiting for a space to become available very close, rather than park just a couple of minutes walk away?

Do you drive your children to school even though it is walking distance to 'save time'?

Do you ask people to bring you things from upstairs to save going up there yourself? If you have to take paperwork to a colleague on another floor in your office, do you wait until there are several items so that you only have to make one journey?

It kind of makes sense doesn't it? Do you recognise yourself in any of these statements? Maybe you are naturally resistant to exercise and probably don't even realise that you're doing it. You'll have to start recognising your resistant behaviour and then make the necessary changes.

Think through your daily activities and note down all the times that you resist exercise and the changes that you could make.

I think increased activity is the key to long term weight loss. There are 168 hours in a week and even if you spent an hour in the gym every single day, you would still have 161 sedentary hours compared with just 7 exercising hours. Let's assume that you sleep for 56 of those hours, leaving you with 105 hours. If we forget about fitness for a minute and just think about energy expenditure, what do you think would be the most beneficial, 105 hours of low level activity or 7 hours of high level activity?

Of course a combination of the two would be the best answer, but you can see how all those little tasks through which you conserve energy, would add up to a bucket load of calories by the end of the week. Remember also the research from week two showed that after an exercise session, your metabolism stays elevated for up to two hours or more, increasing your energy expenditure beyond the cost of the exercise itself. If this is true of specific exercise, it surely must be true of activity too. So, that could add up to two bucket loads of calories! Make a plan now!

Exercise

Aerobic & Anaerobic. What does it really mean?

Here comes the science again.
Aerobic and Anaerobic are two different types of energy systems. Aerobic simply means 'with oxygen' whilst anaerobic means 'without oxygen'.

During exercise, the delivery of oxygen to the exercising muscles takes on a special significance. Oxygen is essential to produce most of the body's energy needs 24 hours a day and most of our body's cells can only produce energy aerobically. For example your heart, nerve and brain tissue cannot function without oxygen. If you do not get enough oxygen to the heart you will have a heart attack and if you do not get enough oxygen to the brain you will suffer a stroke.

However, your muscles have a unique capability of producing energy even when your heart and lungs are unable to produce enough oxygen to meet the energy demand. Our muscles spend the majority of the time in an aerobic state but as you increase the workload from a resting state to an exercising state, the need for oxygen in the muscles increases substantially. As the intensity continues to rise the heart and lungs will reach a point at which they can no longer supply enough oxygen to support aerobic energy production. This is called the anaerobic threshold. Once you cross the anaerobic threshold you will be able to continue exercising for a short time, but anaerobic exercise leads to quick fatigue.

If weight loss is your motivation for exercise, it is important that you work at the correct exercise intensity. You can only use fat as a fuel source if you have enough oxygen present at the muscles and therefore you must stay 'aerobic' throughout your exercise programme.

Aerobic energy uses predominantly fat as a fuel source along with some glucose.

Anaerobic energy uses just glucose as a fuel source.

As the body can only store a small amount of glucose, anaerobic energy can only be sustained for a short length of time. But as we know only too well, our body is capable of storing lots of fat and therefore aerobic energy can be sustained for a very long time.

The most important question then is how will you know when you are working aerobically?

Well, you are actually working aerobically right now whilst you are reading my book and even when you are sleeping. You are getting enough oxygen to the muscles, breathing is easy, you are using fat as fuel and so therefore you are in an aerobic state. Hooray! No wait, it's true that you are working aerobically at the moment but resting isn't a very effective exercise level I'm afraid.

Firstly, aerobic exercise is the type that involves large muscle groups in rhythmical, continuous movements, such as: walking, cycling, swimming, stairclimbing, dancing etc.

Secondly and most commonly, we use heart rates to decide where your aerobic training zone should be. To do this you can take 220 – age = predicted maximum heart rate. Then depending on how fit you are, you should work out at about 60 – 80% of your predicted maximum heart rate. Personally I hate this method. I think it is a vague, sweeping generalisation, like saying that if you are five feet tall you should weigh 8 stone. Most people don't really know how to take their heart rate effectively during exercise and end up stopping what they are doing which drops the heart rate very quickly and can be dangerous. So, try this instead, we know that we have to get enough oxygen to the muscles in order to use fat as a fuel source and the most effective way of doing this is to think about your breathing rate whilst you are exercising.

You should spend about five minutes gradually increasing your heart rate from its resting state to its exercising state so that your heart and lungs can deliver a little more oxygen at a time, rather than putting a big demand on them all at once. Your breathing and heart rate will obviously elevate whilst you do this and you should keep increasing the workload every couple of minutes until you feel that your breathing is laboured, but comfortable.

Your goal is not to cross the anaerobic threshold, where you can no longer use fat as a fuel source. Fortunately, there are some easy ways to recognise the anaerobic threshold:

1. **Breathlessness.** Hyperventilation during exercise is an indication of inadequate oxygen in the exercising muscles and therefore such exercise would be anaerobic. So as soon as your breathing becomes uncomfortable, reduce the intensity of your exercise. In other words slow down!

2. **Burning sensation in the exercising muscles.** The by-product of aerobic energy is carbon dioxide as we breath out and water as we sweat. However, the by-product of anaerobic exercise is lactic acid.

As lactic acid builds up in the muscles it leads to an immediate sense of discomfort and burning in the muscles. If you feel this slow down!

3. **Quick fatigue.** You should be able to continue with aerobic energy for a long time. If you start to feel tired very quickly you are working in the anaerobic training zone. Slow down!

There are 3500 calories in one pound of fat and burning calories at a rate of one per minute at rest means we would have to rest for a very long time in order to burn off just one pound. To realise substantial fat burning, your exercise intensity must be increased well above rest, but stay below the anaerobic threshold.

Strength Training

Do you need to do strength training while you're trying to lose weight? After all, the last thing you want is to build more bulk. The answer... Yes Yes Yes!

Muscle mass is metabolically active. That means that it burns calories for you. Lots and lots and lots of calories. A muscle makes every single tiny move you make with your body and the body has to look after and nurture and feed these muscles with blood and glucose and oxygen and fat!

It is true that when you exercise aerobically you burn lots of calories whilst you are doing it and when you strength train you don't. But, think about all those hours that you are not exercising again. If you had more muscle mass you would be able to burn more calories while you were resting and the best way to get more muscle mass is to strength train.

If you are working out in the gym, ask one of the qualified fitness instructors to show you how to use the weights equipment safely. Or you could take a class. Ask a member of staff which classes are based on strength or toning. This type of class is great as you can rest whenever you like and there is no need to keep up as you are usually standing on the spot or lying on the floor.

The following pages show some strength and flexibility exercises that I have included for you if you wish to start your own programme at home. I have given various levels for you to work through as you become stronger and you should try to do some three times per week. I have included some photos for you to follow of me doing the exercises at different levels.

Use small water bottles for weights and add more water as you get stronger. You should do **three sets of ten of each exercise**. When you can do ten easily, it is time to move to the more advanced level or increase your weights.

The Press Up

This exercise works your chest and triceps at the back of your arms.

There are four levels of intensity for this exercise.

a)   Stand with your feet about twelve inches away from the wall and hip width apart.
Place you hands on the wall a little wider than shoulder width apart.
Hold your stomach in tightly and lower your chest to the wall.
Push away from the wall back to the starting position fully extending the arms.
Repeat.

b)   Take your position on the floor on your hands and knees.
Again, hands are a little wider than shoulder width apart.
Hold your abdominal muscles in tightly, leave your bottom in the air and lower your chest to the floor.
Push away from the floor back to the starting position fully extending the arms. (See picture)
Repeat.

The Press Up (continued)

c)   From all fours position take your hands forwards so that you have a straight line from your shoulders to your knees (see picture).

Hold your abdominal muscles in tightly to support the lower back.

Lower your whole body to the floor not just your chest.

Push away from the floor taking the body back to the start position. Be careful to keep your body in a straight line and don't arch your back.

Repeat.

d)   Take the position up onto your toes.

The Single Arm Row

This exercise works the muscles in your back.

Using a chair, make a square with your body by placing one knee and one hand on it.

Keep your abdominal muscles pulled in tightly to support your back and keep it straight.

Holding your weight, pull it towards you, keeping your elbow bent at a right angle.

Make sure that you keep your shoulders square to the floor and avoid twisting your body.

Concentrate on squeezing the muscles in your back as you make the lift, rather than just using your arm.

Repeat.

To make this exercise harder, you should increase the weight you are lifting.

The Shoulder Press

This exercise works the muscles in your shoulders.

You can do this exercise standing or sitting. Keep your abdominal muscles in tightly to support your back and keep your body in a straight line.
Hold the weights at shoulder height.
Press the weights directly up until the arms are fully extended but the elbows are not locked. Slowly release back down to shoulder height.
Repeat.

The Bicep Curl

This exercise works the biceps in the front of your arm.

Again you can do this exercise standing or sitting. Hold your abdominals in tightly to support your back.
Hold the weights down by your side. Keep your upper arm still and pull your hands up to your shoulders.
Lower the weights back down until your arm is fully extended.
Repeat.

This page is blank for no apparent reason. I was going to make up some excuse about it being for you to write down the weights that you are using and the number of repetitions that you are managing. But the truth is I have no photo to accompany the shoulder press and the bicep curl. I screwed up! But hey, a progress page isn't a bad idea is it?

The Dip

This exercise works the triceps in the back of your arms.

There are two levels of intensity for this exercise.

a)   Sit on the floor with your knees bent and your hands on the
     floor behind you.
     Your fingers should be pointing towards your body.
     Pull your abdominal muscles in and slowly lower your upper
     body down towards the floor by bending your arms.
     Extend the arms to bring you back to the upright position but
     don't lock your elbows. (See picture)
     Repeat.

b)   Sit on the chair with your hands by your sides.   Fingers
     pointing forwards.
     Keeping your knees at a right angle, take your bottom away
     from the chair.
     Slowly lower your body towards the floor by bending your
     elbows.
     Return by extending your arms fully but do not lock your
     elbows.
     Repeat.

The Leg Extension

This exercise works the quadriceps in the front of your thighs.

a)   Lie on your back with your knees bent. Abdominal muscles pulled in tightly.

Extend one leg at a time. Squeeze the muscles in the front of your thigh when the leg is fully extended.

Return the leg to the floor and repeat with the other. (See picture)

Repeat.

b)   Lie on your back again with your knees pulled in towards you. Place your hands just underneath your bottom to support your lower back.

Extend both legs directly up towards the ceiling. Squeeze the thighs when the legs are fully extended.

Repeat.

The Leg Curl

This exercise works the hamstring muscles in the back of the thigh and the gluteus maximus in your bottom.

Hold onto the back of your chair. Extend one leg out behind you. Lean forward slightly so that your back stays in a straight line.

Lift your extended leg a few inches, squeezing your bottom as you do so.

Now lift your heal towards your bottom squeezing the hamstrings in the back of your thigh.

Extend your leg back to the straight position and lower to the floor.

Repeat.

Abdominals

This exercise works the stomach muscles.

a)   Lie face down on the floor with you forehead resting on your hands.

Now take a breath in. You should be able to feel your stomach and abdominal muscles resting on the floor.

As you breathe out pull the abdominal muscles in and up as if you are trying to pull your stomach up off of the floor.

As you do this your should feel your tail bone drop and your back pulling into a straight line.

Repeat.

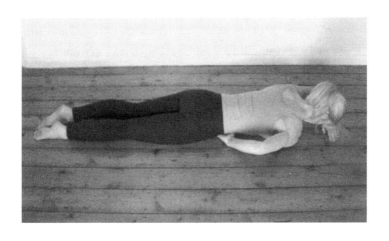

The Abdominal Curl (continued)

b)   Lie on your back with your knees bent and your feet flat on the floor.

Place your hands behind your head to support your head and neck. Lift your elbows slightly so that you can just see them out of the corner of your eyes.

This is the correct position.

Breathe in to prepare and then as you breathe out, pull the abdominal muscles in and up and lift your head and shoulders slightly. You will feel the abdominal muscles contract.

Breathe in as you lower yourself back to the floor and repeat.

If you are unsure of the movement and what you should be feeling, try thinking about it in a slightly different way. My favourite way of describing it, is what happens to my stomach muscles when I am lying on the floor relaxing and I suddenly spot my four-year-old son rushing towards me. My immediate and natural reaction is to contract my abdominal muscles to protect myself as he hurls himself on top of me!

You don't think about it, you just do it to avoid being injured. What would you do if someone were about to punch you in the stomach? Again you would contract the abdominal muscles as hard as you could. Practise and practise. If you are still not sure, bounce a small child on your stomach! You will quickly learn whether you are contracted or not!

Flexibility

Why? Will it make me slimmer? Will it make me fitter? Will it give me more energy? No, No, No. But... It will return the muscles to their normal length after all that contracting whilst you were exercising and it will help to elongate and lengthen your muscles rather than letting them get short, tight and bulky! Definitely a good enough reason, don't you think? And besides, it feels nice and helps you to relax.

You deserve it!   You should hold each stretch for at least 15 – 20 seconds.

The Hamstrings

Back of your thighs.

a)   Lie on your back with you knees bent.
      Pull one or both legs in towards you and slowly extend it/them towards the ceiling.
      It doesn't matter if your legs are bent slightly. You should feel the stretch through the back of your thighs. You should feel slight tension, no pain and if your legs start to shake you have taken it too far. Never ever bounce!
      Release the leg/s back to the floor after 15 – 20 seconds and then repeat with the other leg if necessary.

The Inner Thighs

a)   Sit up with your knees out to the side and the soles of your feet together.

Hold onto your ankles and then take your body weight forwards until you feel a stretch through the inside of your thighs.

b)   You can increase the stretch by extending your legs out to the side. (See picture)

c)   If you want to progress the stretch further, lie down on your back and take both legs into the air as in the hamstring stretch. Slowly lower the legs out to the side, supporting both legs behind the thigh.

Be careful to keep your lower back on the ground. If you feel a gap starting to appear underneath your back your should go back to the previous level.

The Quadriceps

Front of the thigh

Lie on your front with your forehead resting on one hand.
Take the other hand behind you and pull one foot in towards
your bottom.
Press the hip down towards the floor to increase the stretch.

The Back Stretch

Take yourself on to all fours with your hands directly underneath your shoulders and your fingers facing forwards.
Relax your head and pull your stomach in, curling up through the spine.
Pull your shoulder blades apart at the top.
Slowly roll back down through the spine until your back is flat.
Repeat.

The Chest Stretch

Place your hands on your lower back with your fingers pointing towards the floor.

Slowly pull your shoulders and elbows backwards, until you feel a stretch across your chest.

Be careful to keep your stomach in and your back in a straight line.

The Calf Stretch

Standing straight, take a step forwards with one leg and leave the other one behind you with your heal on the floor.

Bend the front leg slightly until you feel a stretch through the lower leg.

Make sure both feet are pointing directly forwards.

Repeat on the other leg.

The Neck Stretch

Standing straight, relax your head down to one side (ear to shoulder).

Extend the opposite arm down and away from you slightly to increase the stretch.

Repeat on the other side.

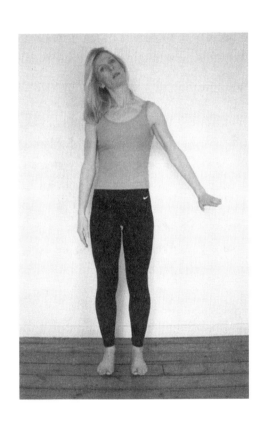

Progression

As you get fitter, you should progress both your cardiovascular and your strength training programme by first increasing your:

Duration – You should be able to exercise aerobically for one hour and you should be able do three sets of ten of your strength exercises. Once you can do this with relative ease you should increase your frequency.

Frequency – You should try to do your aerobic exercises and your strength exercises three times per week. You can do this on alternate days or the same day if you prefer. When you are comfortable with this level of frequency you should increase your intensity.

Intensity – Increase your aerobic intensity by increasing the speed at which you do your chosen exercise or if you are using gym equipment you could increase the resistance.
Increase your strength training intensity by increasing your weights or taking a more advanced position.

Here comes the cliché, but true, oh so true….
It takes perspiration, determination and motivation, but when you've finished a good workout, you don't just feel better, you feel better about yourself.

This Week's Tasks

1. Make a list of all the things that you do to resist exercise or activity.

2. Write a list of all the ways in which you intend to increase your general activity. Put it into practice straight away.

3. If you haven't already, make a plan for specific exercise and write it in your diary on a weekly basis. Start now.

4. Think carefully about your exercise intensity when you are working out this week. Remember your breathing should be laboured but comfortable (not gasping)! If you are not sure whether you are working hard enough take it up a notch and see what happens. Above all, work at your own pace doing something that you enjoy and don't try to keep up with anybody else.

5. If you are not already doing some resistance training start to incorporate some of the exercises I have shown you to increase your strength and muscle density. You should aim to do 20 minutes resistance training three times per week. It is an ideal way to increase your activity on the days that you are not doing any cardiovascular training.

6. Make your own short term goals, based on the weeks upcoming events. Plan, Plan, Plan!

7. Make sure that you have an hour to spare before beginning next week's chapter. There is a time consuming task to complete.

This Week's Goals
(Make at least one but not more than five)

➢ .

➢ .

➢ .

➢ .

➢ .

Notes…

Week Five

Week five already. You have nearly completed the learning phase of your programme. Go and get a pen and don't read on until you've got one. Hey, I said go and get a pen! With only one more week to go, you need to start making plans that will help you to continue with the programme.

Take a look back at all the task lists and short-term goals that you have used to help you over the last few weeks.

Make a list of your three most important ongoing short-term goals.

_____

_____

_____

Have a quick think about your pre programme eating habits.
List six positive changes to your eating habits since beginning your Weigh Of Life programme.

_____

_____

_____

_____

_____

_____

Make four lists and time yourself how long it takes you to complete the task. Your time starts as soon as you have read the questions.

a) Write down 5 things that you physically like about yourself.
b) Write down 5 things that you are good at.
c) Write down 5 achievements that you have made in your life.
d) Write down 5 things that you think other people like about you.

Now make four more lists. Again time yourself to see how long it takes

a) Write down 5 things that you don't physically like about yourself.
b) Write down 5 things that you are not very good at.
c) Write down 5 things that you would like to have achieved but haven't so far.
d) Of those 5 things list the ones that you think you still might achieve at some point.

Positive Lists

a) Five things that I physically like about myself

1._____

2._____

3._____

4._____

5._____

b) Five things that I am good at

1._____

2._____

3._____

4._____

5._____

c) Five achievements that I have made in my life

1._____

2._____

3._____

4._____

5._____

d) Five things that I think other people like about me

1._____

2._____

3._____

4._____

5._____

Negative Lists

a) Five things that I don't physically like about myself

1._____

2._____

3._____

4._____

5._____

b) Five things that I am not very good at

1._____

2._____

3._____

4._____

5._____

c) Five things that I would have liked to achieve but haven't

1._____

2._____

3._____

4._____

5._____

d) Five things that I think I might still achieve at some point

1._____

2._____

3._____

4._____

5._____

This is quite a difficult task, but it's great isn't it? It shows up a clear indication of how positive or negative you are about yourself. I got the idea from an Oprah show years ago. Except she had a guest who suggested that you write down all of the things that you are, for example: mother, sister, daughter, friend, wife, lover, housekeeper etc. and then to make notes on how well you are doing in each area and how you can become a better person. She suggested that you give yourself marks out of ten for each relevant role that you had

148

played on a daily basis. Well good idea in theory perhaps, but honestly, it made me feel like a totally inadequate failure on many levels!!

Everyone in the world who has kids knows that guilt plays a major part in your role as a parent. I haven't seen my brother for weeks, because he's as busy as I am. My mum helps me out ten thousand times more than I have ever helped her (I really must show more appreciation). My friends catch up with me when they can. My husband gets dinner on the table most nights (does that count as being a good wife)? And being a good lover at midnight when the football has finally finished and he decides to come to bed isn't always easy. Finally, the house is always spotless so long as you don't turn up unannounced!

I tried it for a week and felt like a miserable failure at the end of the task. But I do think I learnt how to become a better person. I was a bit like a first time exerciser trying to do everything at once and hating every minute of it. Now I think things through more rationally. I am a good friend and sometimes I think that's all that matters. I can be a good friend to my children, husband, parents and brother as well and so long as I am there when they really need me, it's a good start. Anyway enough of that. Have you done your lists yet?

Don't worry if it's taking a long time. If it has taken you longer to do the positive lists than the negative ones, it simply shows that you usually have negative thoughts first. But over the next couple of weeks you're going to try to turn it around and learn how to think more positively. Now that you have written some positive things about yourself, keep reminding yourself of them every day and have fun adding to them.

This week we are going to look at different types of self-control and responsibility, along with rational and irrational thoughts that may be standing in the way of your success. It is also time to take a quick recap over your general eating habits to check whether you have a basic nutritional balance.

Taking Responsibility for Your Actions

Self-control (we've all got some somewhere) is the ability to achieve the goals that we set ourselves (so make them easy)! and along with control comes responsibility (unfortunately). After all, you are the only person that actually puts food into your mouth (usually). In order to maintain control your thoughts must be positive and rational. You have to believe in your ability to control difficult situations.

Have you heard of the British athlete Roger Bannister? He was the first person to run a mile in less than four minutes. Although it was a task that nobody had ever achieved previously, many runners achieved the same success in the following months. It is
now widely accepted by experts that a psychological barrier had been broken down and once these other athletes believed it was possible, they too went on to break the four-minute barrier. The only

change from their previous attempts was that now they believed they could.

We think and behave in a way that is consistent with our beliefs. If you have many failed weight loss attempts behind you, your beliefs regarding your ability may be hampering your success. We will be looking at positive and negative thoughts next week and I have included some tasks for you to do this week in preparation.

First take a look at these two different types of control:

Internal Control

Internal control comes from within your own thoughts and feelings and in order to be successful you need to train yourself to think positively and rationally. You can't do this unless you can first recognise the negative or irrational thoughts that you may have.

An example of a very common irrational statement is "if I lose weight, I'll be happier" Ask yourself why you think you will be happier at a lower weight. What could you achieve at a lower weight that you cannot achieve now? Would those achievements make you completely happy? Would your happiness be directly related to your body weight? You should try to analyse your irrational thoughts and put them into a positive and more rational perspective. It is true that you may be more confident and outgoing and feel great about yourself, but most likely everything else in your life will be much the same. Don't put so much pressure on yourself and overlook the things that are already very happy in your life even though you are heavier than you would like.

Here's another good example, my friend did it to me just the other day.
We had arranged to meet for lunch at 1.00pm. But then she had to wait for a delivery and we re-arranged the time to 3.00pm. We didn't communicate properly and I thought that we were still meeting for lunch, whilst she thought that because it was much later we would just be meeting for a drink. Therefore she had eaten and I hadn't. She kept apologising and when I had finished my meal and decided to have dessert, she said "I'll have a dessert too because I feel bad that you have had to eat alone". I quickly explained that I wanted to have dessert but I didn't care at all if she didn't. She insisted.

She had done a classic "If I don't have a dessert, my dinner partner will feel uncomfortable". This is a completely irrational thought and a blatant excuse to have a dessert, but she genuinely believed that it would make me feel better. You must not allow yourself to become responsible for other people's feelings. Ask yourself if you care more about your dinner partner's feelings toward dessert or your efforts to become slimmer stronger and healthier?
Rationalise your thoughts I promise you, they don't care whether you have dessert or not.

This also works in reverse

"Nobody else is having dessert, so I can't either because they will think that I'm fat and greedy". Will they? Or is that what you think of yourself and therefore assume other people are thinking it too? This is a negative and irrational thought. You know now that it is not a single dessert that will make you gain weight, but long term eating behaviour and patterns. Now that you have changed these you can enjoy many low fat desserts without damaging your programme. You are getting leaner and fitter and stronger and if you want to have a dessert, do so, safe in the knowledge that you body is changing for the better and who cares what your dinner partner thinks?!

You must try to recognise your irrational and negative thoughts before you can start work on changing them.

One of my clients changed her whole lifestyle around, by just changing one huge irrational thought. Although she was invited out to social events on at least three or four nights of the week, she rarely went as many of the events involved eating. She felt embarrassed to eat with her friends and colleagues as she thought everyone would be watching her to see why she was fat. Instead she would go home alone and eat.

After some gentle persuasion from me and a few checked menus so that she was confident about what she was eating, she decided to accept a few invitations.

Her whole attitude changed within weeks. She now never passes up an invitation. She quickly realised that nobody cared what she was eating as they were all too busy making their own choices to notice. She started to enjoy herself more and more, she was no longer home alone in the danger zone (the kitchen!) and the weight started to fall off. She says it is only now that people are interested in what she is eating, because they can't understand how she is eating so much and the weight is still coming off! By changing her irrational thoughts, she's now happy, sociable, slimmer and rarely at home.

External Control

External control comes from outside sources: peer pressure; situations such as visiting friends or family; eating out in a restaurant; somebody's birthday at work and they are buying cream cakes for everyone; a member of the family snacking on
chocolate (you weren't thinking about chocolate a moment ago but now you are desperate for it!) You know the kind of thing.

If you recognise yourself here, you are probably an external person. Some studies have shown that overweightness can be directly related to externality and that these people regularly blame their success or failure on things or people other than themselves.
You need to think through every situation and make a plan of how you are going to deal with it next time it happens. Here are some examples. Get your highlighter pen again and mark off the ones that might work for you or add them to your intervention plan.

When visiting friends or family that are offering you biscuits.
"No thank you, I've just eaten or "No thank you, but would you mind if I had a sandwich" Don't debate whether to have it or not or

they will pressure you. Always answer quickly and don't give yourself time to think about whether you want it or not.

Eating in a restaurant. You should have a great plan for this one by now, a whole list of tips is included in week three..

A birthday at work. "I've gone off cream, would you mind if I had an iced bun Instead?" (they are usually low in fat) or "I'm not feeling too good actually, maybe I'll have one later" They will have forgotten or somebody else will have eaten it by then. Keep a fruit bowl or low fat snacks in your desk so you always have something to snack on.

Seeing someone snacking on chocolate. I'm the expert on this one! Keep some fun size chocolate bars in the freezer. This way, when you are craving it you can have a small bar, which will take you a long time to eat and still taste as good. Keeping them in the freezer also keeps them out of sight and makes it very difficult to binge on them in a moment of madness without breaking your teeth! You could try a time delay. Tell yourself that you only want the chocolate because you've just seen someone else with it. If you still want it in an hour then you will allow yourself a small piece. Or distraction. Go for a walk, phone a friend, write a letter, take a bath or ask yourself "do I want it, more than I want to be slim?"

I strongly believe that if you really love a food that is high in fat, like chocolate, you must not deny yourself it completely (convenient that!) If you tell yourself that you can't have something you will want it even more. Take this example. You have an apple and a kit kat in front of you and you really want the kit kat. You have the apple. Half an hour later you have the kit kat also! You spent that half an hour craving the kit kat and trying desperately to resist. When you finally give in you feel a huge sense of failure and lack of control and beat yourself up about it for the rest of the day! (I've been there many times) Next time, make a conscious decision about how you might feel if you have it and how you might feel if you resist. If you decide to have it, enjoy it, don't look back and then get straight back on your programme.

Do not let externalities take control!

Eat a Variety of Foods From
Each Group Every Day

Since you've been making changes to your eating habits for a few weeks now, it is a good idea to do a quick check and make sure that your diet is sill nutritionally balanced. These are general nutritional guidelines for the four basic food groups. Take a look and check to make sure that you are still within the guideline for each group every day.

Milk and Milk Products (dairy)
Children up to 11 years 2-3 servings
Adolescents 3-4 servings
Pregnant and nursing women 3-4 servings
Adults 2 servings
For example ½ a pint of milk or two yoghurts

Meat, Fish, Poultry and Alternatives

2 servings

For example, beans at lunch time and fish with your evening meal

Breads and Cereals

Wholegrain and enriched. 3-5 servings

For example, carbohydrates at every meal. This group includes pasta and rice.

Fruits and vegetables

Include at least two vegetables 4-5 servings

For example, 2 fruit snacks and a mixed salad with dinner incorporating tomatoes, cucumber and mixed leaves

If you notice any areas in which you are lacking, make a note on your goal sheet for this week and see if you can rectify the problem. Women should pay particular attention to milk and dairy products to ensure sufficient calcium intake and avoid such conditions as osteoporosis.

This Week's Tasks

1. Go back over all the previous week's tasks and short-term goals that you have made and make sure that they are all still being achieved.

2. Make a conscious effort this week to recognise all negative thoughts, not just the ones that are related to your programme or your body image. Constantly change them into positive thoughts. If you can't think of a positive alternative, write down the negative thought. You will probably be able to think of one later when you are feeling more positive.

3. Make a conscious effort to notice as many cars that are the same as yours this week. (a strange request, but all will be revealed next week).

4. Remember your positive and negative lists? Ask someone close to you to complete the first four lists and time how long it takes them. I have left the following pages blank for them to do this. Then compare their answers to yours.

a) 5 things they physically like about you.

b) 5 things that they think you are good at.

c) 5 achievements that they think you have made.

d) 5 things that they think other people like about you.

Be prepared to be surprised by the results!

This Week's Goals

(Make at least one but not more than five)

➤ .

➤ .

➤ .

➤ .

➤ .

Notes…

Week six

This is the last chapter of the book. But nowhere near the end of your Weigh of Life programme. In fact, there is no end. I hope that the principles that you've learned over the last six weeks will be with you forever, except that once you are as fit and as healthy and slim and strong as you want to be, you will just be a little more relaxed about your choices. I'll let you into a secret now, although you may have worked it out for yourself already. The healthy eating guidelines that I quoted you at the beginning of the book are correct and you have been sticking to 30% fat or less. However, I have been getting you to check product labels and stay below 30% per product. In reality, this way of calculating your fat intake would hold your overall intake on a daily or weekly basis at much lower than 30%. Once you've lost all the weight you want to lose (and only then) you can loosen up a little. You still want to stay below 30%ish to ensure a healthy level of fat, but you can calculate it with a much more open mind.

For example, if you want sausages (they are usually about 60% fat or more) you could serve them with some very low fat options such as stir fried with peppers, onions, garlic, mushrooms, fresh chopped tomatoes, fresh basil and served on a bed of pasta. Because there is virtually no fat in the rest of the ingredients, the total composition of the meal would be less than 30%. But obviously if you serve them with creamed mashed potato and gravy the total amount of fat for the meal would hit the roof! So you can juggle things around a little. Don't be paranoid about every single thing being low fat and don't spend time trying to calculate every calorie and fat gram to make sure you haven't gone overboard. Just eat sensibly, eat loads and feel great.

Now that this is the last week that you are going to be supported by the book, It is a good time to start making more plans for your continued success. Think about the major things that have kept you motivated so far and how you can stay motivated in the future.

. Here are some examples. Go get that highlighter pen again and then add them to your intervention plan:

- Plan ahead. Think about the next event that is coming up and what you might like to wear for it.

- Get a friend to join you in your weight loss efforts for some moral support.

- Get your family to sponsor you for your favourite charity.

- Go back to the beginning of your Weigh of Life book and begin the task lists again

- Continue to make your short-term goals every week. Think about what is happening in the coming week that might make things difficult for you and make an action plan. (do this one for sure).

- Step up your exercise efforts to kick your metabolism.

- Make yourself a big graph of your success to stick inside the kitchen cupboards. I had a client that stuck a drawing of a Christmas tree on the wall with eight branches. In the run up to Christmas she had her children make decorations to stick on the branches everytime she lost a pound. The pressure was on from the children to get the fairy on the top before the big day!

- Take up a new hobby to keep you busy and take your mind off food.

These are just a few ideas that might help you. Make a list of your own too and then put some of them into action. It doesn't matter how strange they are. I once had a client who had lost 3 stone but still needed to lose the last 7 pounds. She was finding it difficult and so gave me £700 on the agreement that I would give her £100 back everytime she lost a pound. If she didn't lose the weight, she wouldn't get her money back. She lost it in three weeks!

Another client was a member of the Conservative Party and made a goal to lose one pound per week. If he didn't achieve his goal, he made himself give money to the Labour Party!

I know you have probably found the constant goal setting and list writing and tasks and action plans etc etc a little tedious. But it is such a very very important part of the programme and I honestly believe that my own success at getting my life back on track and learning to love food rather than view it as the enemy, came from understanding myself better. Putting time and thought into my behaviour, making written plans of change and putting those plans into action when the going got tough. Make it different from anything that you've done before. Learn about yourself and succeed where you've previously failed. It's the best feeling in the world.

It took a lot of effort and strained several relationships along the way, especially my relationship with my parents. They knew that I was unhappy and struggling with my food and exercise obsessions, but they didn't know how to help me. I thought they were ganging up on me and interfering. They were at their wits' end with worry and nothing they seemed to do or say made any difference.

Then when I left home and moved to Milton Keynes, I shared a house with a guy called Matt. He was the manager at the health club where I was working. He seemed like a nice guy at first, but things quickly changed. He called me into his office one day and told me that he thought I was a fantastic instructor, a brilliant motivator and that several members had commented on how I was a great asset to the team. I was thrilled. But as he continued, he said that while he was happy with my work, he didn't think I was a good role model for the members. I was painfully thin, exercising too much and up one minute and down the next. "Sort yourself out and I will help you if you like, otherwise I will no longer continue to have you working here". I was devastated, I was angry and I was bitter. How dare he tell me that the members thought I was great and then tell me he was going to fire me if I didn't gain weight. I threw several obscenities at him (I am eternally grateful that he didn't sack me there and then) and slammed the door as hard as I could on the way out.

The next day, he called me back into his office and told me that I was no longer allowed to exercise in the gym or participate in classes. I would only be allowed to teach three classes per week, all of which were fairly static relaxation or strength classes. Also I would not be allowed to teach on the weight control programmes that were running in the club and instead I would have to run the cholesterol-screening programme. "Oh my God" He had turned into the devil himself.

I didn't speak to him for three weeks even though we were living in the same house. But I did learn everything I could ever wish to know about cholesterol. I ran a fantastic screening programme which made a lot of profit for the club and I proved that I was a very valuable staff member regardless of my craziness.

I was still angry with Matt until one day he didn't show up for work. I discovered later from his girlfriend that he had been rushed to hospital to have his appendix removed. Late that night I went to the hospital and convinced the nurse (who was a member at the club, fortunately) to let me see him for just one minute. She did but told me not to make any noise as it was so late and not to wake him as he needed rest after his operation.

I went to his bed, held his hand for thirty seconds and then left. He didn't even know that I was there.

That night I lay awake for hours trying to make sense of my actions. Why did I do that? I didn't even like him.

It's difficult to remember how I analysed it at the time, it was eleven years ago after all, but I do know that from that moment I had realised that Matt wasn't being nasty to me, he was trying to help. Deep down I must have realised that and I wanted to be there for

166

him too. The next day I saw the mission statement that I have included for you in week two.

I started to think about what I was doing in a very different light and I decided to make that day, day one of my plan to get healthy. It wasn't easy and I'm telling you that because I think that whatever you're trying to achieve with regard to your body image, it is never easy. However many headlines you see saying 'lose a stone in a week it's so easy' we all know that it's a pile of lies really. Good days, bad days, up days, down days, easy days, and hard days. That's the reality. It took a long time but I had been unhappy with my body for a long time, so a quick fix wasn't what I was looking for. It was long term success.

Now you might wonder how I came to end up spending the rest of my career helping people to lose weight when I've never been overweight myself and many will say "huh! What does she know about being overweight?" Maybe not enough, but I have had massive success in helping people lose weight. I think that is because I have a very clear understanding of the emotional turmoil that can be caused when you are unhappy with your body and I know that when you can channel those emotions into something more positive, success is the only outcome.

Take Sally for example, Sally is the young girl that I have quoted on the back cover of the book. When I first met her, I saw the desperation in her eyes, desperation after four years of obsessing about her weight, her body, exercise, calories. I'd never met her before, we had a brief chat and then the next day her mum called me and said "You met my daughter last night and I don't know what you said to her, but please will you come to our house and talk to her some more". Whatever I'd said, Sally was ready to change, ready to re-channel her thoughts, stop being negative and start living a 'normal' life. I saw Sally last night. I went to her house to ask her for a few words to put on the back cover. She's doing really well, she has a little further to go yet, but she's strong, she's happy, she's confident and she's positive. There is no doubt in my mind that she is going to make it all the way.

Here is the last mission statement. I love the mission statements, all the ones that I have included for you in this book have helped me become what I am today. Unfortunately, as I kind of picked them up along my way through life, I have no idea who the authors are. If anybody out there does recognise them please let me know as I would love to give them some recognition.

Believe in yourself
Have fun
Enjoy the process
and
Do what it takes
to get the job done

This last chapter is about sticking with your goals and your intervention plans, regardless of what else happens in your life. You can't plan to lose weight this year and not encounter anything that will throw you off track. It will be a challenge on a daily basis and you need to learn some problem solving skills along the way.

Sticking With It - Adherence to the Programme

Most people attempting to make behaviour changes rarely find that their new behaviour becomes habit in the short term. In the early stages of change, you may (subconsciously) continually debate with yourself about whether or not to continue with the programme. Even standing in the kitchen debating whether or not to eat the leftover dessert could be considered this kind of subconscious debate. This does not mean that you lack motivation or skill, but that you are assessing environmental changes and current feelings, for example, unexpected problems or demands, fear, anger, depression, illness etc. All can potentially threaten your decision to continue. If you've had a rough day, you may be telling yourself that you deserve it. You will have to learn how to challenge or distract yourself from these kinds of thoughts.

Many of the changes required to stick with the programme have negative factors, for example, time and effort required, disruption of usual food preparation, keeping records, finding time to exercise etc. How you weigh up these negative factors against the more long-term positive factors are essential to the success of the programme.

Many influences that affect your decision will be relatively **stable**. These will include your new-found knowledge, your progression through the programme, your expected outcomes and your success so far.

Other influences are more **fluid**, including your emotional, psychological and physical States. These are sure to change on a daily basis.

Fluid factors can change regularly, becoming stronger and weaker, and may have a strong effect on your decision to continue.

You must find ways of reducing the negative factors and promoting the positive factors.

One of the best ways to do this is to use problem-solving skills.

a) Identify the problem. For example, your desk being next to a vending machine at work.
b) Writing down alternative solutions. For example, ask to have your desk moved, take no money with you, ask for some healthy snacks to be sold in the vending machine, take your own snacks with you so that you don't need to use the vending machine.
c) Weighing the likelihood of success for each solution.
d) Trying one solution.
e) Assessing its effects.
f) Revising the solution if necessary. If it doesn't work, don't give up keep looking for ways to make life easier.

Alternatively, make a list of all the reasons to continue and then a list of reasons that you shouldn't continue. This will help you to reinforce your long-term goals and keep you focused on your wish to be slim.

Make sure that you allow yourself some space from your programme when necessary; remember the shades of grey that we talked about during week one rather than seeing things in black and white (on it or off it). Christmas and holidays are an example. Nobody wants to be trying to lose weight at times like this and your goals at these times should be based around maintaining your weight. Increasing your exercise and choosing sensibly where you can, whilst treating yourself and not missing out at the same time. So long as your weight never goes up you are still winning. It is ok to put your programme on hold occasionally but plan a date to start losing again and stick to it!

Negative beliefs and their effects

We know that people who have failed to lose weight on numerous occasions previously usually hold negative beliefs about their ability to control their eating habits and regularly blame themselves for their weight problem. The consequences of this are lower self-esteem, a sense of helplessness and a negative attitude. All the feelings that will certainly stand in their way again next time. If you are to overcome your weight problems, you must overcome your negativity first.

You'll remember that last week I set you the task of noticing as many cars as you can that are the same as yours .

Have you ever brought a new car and then suddenly become aware of just how many of them are around?

I remember walking in town one day having recently discovered that I was pregnant and every other woman seemed to be pregnant also. In fact I was quite amazed at how many, as I had never noticed it before.

Why does this happen and what possible relevance can this have to your weight loss programme?

It is because of the reticular activating system (R.A.S). Everybody has one and it is a little cluster of brain cells that acts as a filter to your perceptions. This cluster of brain cells filters in information that is consistent with your beliefs and goals and at the same time filters out any irrelevant information. As you can imagine, we are capable of taking in millions and millions of bits of information and if our brain allowed it, we would simply be overwhelmed. The reticular activating system prevents that from happening.

Do you see where I am heading with this? If you have negative beliefs about yourself and your abilities, your brain will keep reinforcing them by only letting in the relevant information that is consistent with your thoughts. Therefore leading you to become more and more negative and behaving more and more consistently with your negative beliefs.

Let's take a look at some examples of this:

Negative	Positive
Self Talk (belief)	**Self Talk (belief)**
"Its too hard, it won't do any good I'll fail anyway".	"I can learn to change my eating habits.
Perception of that belief	**Perception of that belief**
"I have no self control, I cannot follow through, so I won't see results".	"Self Control is a skill that I can develop with practice".
Feelings	**Feelings**
Anxious, overwhelmed, Feel like eating.	Energetic, capable, in control.
Behaviour	**Behaviour**
When thinking of eating, goes for a short walk and eats on return.	Plans ahead and goes for walk after dinner, instead of having dessert.
Reinforcement	**Reinforcement**
" It was too hard, it didn't work I knew I would fail"	"I can be in control and change my behaviour".

The negative person in this example is trying very hard, but does not really believe that they are capable of sticking with the necessary changes. They know that they should go for a walk instead of eating in order to distract themselves. But they eat on return because they didn't really expect themselves to succeed and so they behave consistently with their negative beliefs and justify it to themselves by saying, "I knew I couldn't do it anyway".

Alternatively, the positive person is telling himself or herself that they can do it. Even if they have failed many times before, they believe that this time it will be different. They feel confident and in control and their behaviour reinforces this. They succeed because they thought they could.

It is not easy to suddenly change all your negative beliefs into positive ones. It takes practice and time. A very effective way to start is by using positive affirmations on a regular basis. An affirmation is a word or phrase that you regularly use to promote positive thought. Such as:

> I am a strong, confident person.
> I am good at this.
> I am getting slimmer.
> I do not fail when I set my mind to something

Let's look at another example of a positive person versus and negative person after going out for dinner with friends and avoiding all temptation by eating a well balanced healthy low fat meal.

Negative	Positive
"It was a fluke"	"That is what I can do
"That's not like me"	consistantly".

"It was a one-off"	"I am good at staying
"I couldn't do it again"	in control"
	"I will definitely do that
	again"

Think about the situations that you find difficult and some affirmations that may help you. Say it to yourself at least 10 times a day.

Let's then imagine that you come up against your first difficult situation after practising your affirmations and it doesn't go according to plan. What will you say to yourself?

Negative	**Positive**
"That's typical"	"That was a one-off"
"I am just not capable"	"I am capable of much more"
"I always behave like that"	"I am better than that"
"I'll be the same next time"	"I'll be much better next time"

You must learn not to be so critical of yourself if you are to become more positive. Look for the positive things that you have achieved every day and make a note in your diary of the things that you are grateful for.

Today is a very happy day for me as I am about to finish my book. I am grateful for all the help that I've received along the way from my family and friends and all the people that have supported me through the ups and downs. Shortly after the beginning of my mission to stop letting food and exercise obsessions control my life, Matt moved to Manchester, then Newcastle and Glasgow. We pretty much lost touch for several years, I heard news of him occasionally through the grapevine and we spoke a couple of times on the phone briefly.

Although I had realised that Matt was the best friend I could have wished for at that time in my life, I still struggled with the way in which he went about helping me. I had spent a lot of time despising him for trying to control me and I didn't miss him when he left. I was working hard to get strong, get positive, get healthy and change my whole relationship with food. I started my own business, I was studying, I moved house and I got married.

My marriage failed within eight months and there began the next most traumatic phase in my life. Matt had returned from the north by then and there he was again lending a shoulder to cry on, giving advice (that I sometimes didn't wish to hear) and generally being a fantastic friend. As he supported me through the ordeal our relationship developed and today we are a strong, committed, happy family with two beautiful children aged 5 and 18 months. I am very happy, very healthy and very fit. I still exercise about four times per week, but I do it because I want to and because I genuinely enjoy it. My metabolism is high and healthy because I never starve my body (my friends would vouch for that!) I don't do any exercise when I go on holiday and I overeat at Christmas, the same as the rest of the world, but hey, life is for living.

My life is balanced and yours can be too.

Good luck.

Tasks For The Coming Weeks

1. Try some affirmations and say them to yourself ten times a day. "I am in control" is a good one to start with.

2. Re-evaluate your long-term goals. Mark them off as soon as they have been achieved and set new ones.

3. Throw or give away any clothes that become too big. You are making a commitment never to return to such a size and therefore you will not need the clothes. When you reach your desired weight or clothes size you will maintain it. If you feel your clothes starting to get tight, you jump straight back into your programme until they are comfortable again. This will only take a week or two. If you have the temptation to just slip into the next size up in your wardrobe, it will be easy to let things get out of hand.

4. Remember that calories still matter. There are many cakes, biscuits and desserts in the supermarket that are low fat and can be regularly included in your programme, but keep things in perspective. Research shows that people eating low fat foods often allow themselves more because of the low fat content. If your weight loss slows down check that you are not over consuming these kinds of products.

5. Plan, Plan, and Plan! Every few weeks keep a food diary again just to keep a closer check on your intake and behaviour.

This Week's Goals

(Make at least one but not more than five)

➢ .

➢ .

➢ .

➢ .

➢ .

Notes…

Surviving Christmas and Holidays

When Christmas is fast approaching all thoughts turn to food and parties and food and shopping and food and family and food and drink! and food!!!

It seems that every social occasion is based around food and drink at this time of year, even a quick 'Hi' to a neighbour can somehow turn into a drink and a mince pie.

You may still be trying to lose last year's excesses.

So, this year it's time to make a plan – one great big plan that will see you through to New Year, taking in all your social outings over the Christmas period, the big dinner and all the endless leftovers without gaining an ounce!

When I say without gaining an ounce that is exactly what I mean. I'm not talking about losing weight, that's definitely not the way to enjoy Christmas, but starting the new year without a bigger problem to tackle will leave you feeling smug and ready to get back on track from January 1st.

So, here's the plan:

1. Go through your diary and look at all the planned social occasions that you have over the Christmas period that are bound to involve a lot of food and drink. List them on a Christmas planning chart (you could just use a calendar) along with your plans for each occasion.

2. Have a think about which ones are likely to be the most difficult and which ones will be easier to choose lower fat healthier options.

3. Choose five days over the entire Christmas period up to New Year's Day on which you will choose to eat whatever you like and then make a plan to stay on track and eat sensibly the rest of the time. (They must not be five consecutive days).

4. Have a look at your 'eating out' notes contained in week four. Follow as many of the guidelines as you can.

5. Christmas dinner itself should be easy if you are the one doing the cooking. Turkey is low fat meat, you can make your stuffing separately and if you omit the sausage meat you can make the stuffing low fat. Use spray light to roast your potatoes and root veg and pile your plate high with other steamed vegetables. Choose cranberry rather than bread sauce and make your gravy with granules rather than meat juices and your dinner will be perfectly acceptable.

Even Christmas pudding is low fat so long as you don't smother it in brandy butter or double cream. Use single cream to complement or if you're not even that keen on Christmas pudding, serve a wonderfully light sorbet for dessert instead.

If you usually have a starter, opt for a fruit based starter like melon with a raspberry coulis.

6. If you are eating Christmas dinner cooked by somebody else, limit the amount of roast potatoes that you have and fill your plate with plenty of vegetables and turkey. Unless of course Christmas day is one of your five chosen 'eat what I like' days.

7. If you have been invited to a friend's house for drinks, take along some low fat 'nibbles' with you. It is not strange at all to go to such a get together and take along a bottle of wine, so nobody will think it odd if you take some pretzels or twiglets or some other low fat snack either. That way if there are bowls or crisps and nuts lying around you won't be tempted and you won't feel left out either.

8. Never tell anyone that you are 'on a diet', or following any type of weight maintenance plan over the Christmas period. This will result in other people trying to pressure you to ease their own conscience and to see how strong willed you are.

9. If you are attending a buffet, eat before you go and avoid it, or if it's at a friend's house, you could take a low fat contribution. Most buffet type foods are very high in fat.

10. Don't overbuy! Two months prior to Christmas, I have seen people loading their trolleys high with mountains of biscuits, sweets, crisps and nuts. Think about how much entertaining you will be doing over the Christmas period and just buy what you need for each occasion. If the children want to have chocolates around the house, buy them selection boxes or a small box of Christmas chocolates. If you think rationally, it is rarely necessary to have a 2kg tin in the

house! By doing this you will limit the amount of leftover Christmas food which will disrupt your efforts to get back on track come January 1st. Remember the shops are only closed for two days and the inconvenience of going to the supermarket more than once is less than that of having an extra half a stone to lose by January because you finished up all the leftovers!

11. Try to stay active over the Christmas period; there should be plenty of opportunity to have a dance at parties or family get-togethers. Or stick some music on to dance with the kids; encourage the whole family to go for a walk before or after dinner. (You've got more chance of getting them to agree before dinner). Or bring out a game of twister to get everyone on their feet. Take yourself off for a swim between Christmas and New Year and relax as you swim up and down (don't take the kids! Use it as an escape and time for yourself).

12. Plan, Plan, Plan every day and stick with your plans. If you go off the rails one day, resist thinking that you will make that one of your five days if you have already allocated it to a day when you know it will be difficult because you are eating with friends. You will use it as a licence to eat badly for the rest of the day and will still have to face the difficult day. You will end up overeating on both days, feeling bad about yourself and spoiling the enjoyment of Christmas. Remember that your chosen five days are days on which you will eat what you fancy within reason, but don't use it as an excuse to eat an entire tin of quality street!

13. Now the big one….ALCOHOL… It stimulates your appetite! And affects your brain so that you don't care!

Plan your high alcohol days in the same way as your food. Try to avoid having days where you consume excesses of alcohol and food on the same day.

For each event where you are likely to drink, make a plan and stick with it. Here are some tips for damage limitation:

➤ Offer to drive. The perfect excuse, nobody will pressure you and you won't change your mind once you are there.

➤ Have a soft drink every other round so that you consume only half the amount of alcohol as others

➤ Dilute wine with soda water to cut the amount that you consume by half (I don't drink and somebody once told me that this was a ludicrous suggestion)!

➤ If you are drinking at home, stick to pub measures so that you can keep track of how much you've had. It is easy to pour doubles or even triples at home.

➤ Decide in advance how many drinks you are going to have and stick with it.

➤ Drink only on social occasions and stick to soft drinks at home.

➤ Make an alcohol bank, decide how many drinks you are going to have for the week and use them up as you go through the week. You could have for example two every day or four on one day and none the next. A good guideline to stick to is the recommended units per week, which are 14 for a woman and 21 for a man.

Have Fun!

Take a look at this sample of two different types of menu for a restaurant meal.

Although at Weigh of Life we don't spend valuable time counting calories, I have listed them here for this example so that you can fully appreciate the difference between the two menus.

Menu 1	Cals	Menu 2	Cals
Whitebait fried in batter	600	Prawn Cocktail	345
Rump steak with	660	Chicken casserole	160
Pepper sauce		New potatoes	60
French Fries	210	French beans	4
Peas	20		
Queen pudding	480	Fresh Fruit Salad	88
Custard	90		
Stilton, biscuits & butter		Camembert & biscuits	
	570		270
Coffee & cream one sugar		Black coffee	
	60		2

Total Calories consumed

	Menu 1	Menu 2
	2690	930

Quite a difference! With menu one most people would gain weight even if they did not consume anything else for the rest of the day, and that doesn't even include drinks!

Check this one out as an example of the average day in the office:

Menu 1	Cals	Menu 2	Cals
Snack		**Snack**	
Tea with milk and sugar	50	Black coffee/lemon tea	4
2 chocolate biscuits	200	1 digestive biscuit	80
Lunch		**Lunch**	
White roll with chicken		wholemeal roll with	
And mayonnaise		cottage cheese and chives	
	390		147
Cream of tomato soup	308	minestrone soup	156
Chocolate éclair	155	Banana	70
Coca cola	88	Diet Coke	1
Snack		**Snack**	
Tea with milk and sugar	50	Black coffee/lemon tea	4
2 chocolate biscuits	200	1 digestive	80

Total calories consumed

Menu 1	Menu 2
1441	**542**

It is easy to see how the calories can soon add up even though it seems that a similar amount of food has been consumed. I have deliberately chosen high fat choices for menu 1 and low fat for menu 2. Remember if you look after the fat the calories will look after themselves. (Although beware the low fat cakes and biscuits available. They are preferable to their high fat counterparts but still contain a lot of calories so be sensible with your treats).

Poor choices at a buffet	**Good choices at a buffet**
Mini pork pie	Piece of crusty bread
Slice of quiche	Chicken pieces(skin removed)
Tortilla chips	Salsa dip
Cheese and pickle sandwich	Ham salad sandwich
Handful of peanuts	Crudites
Small garlic bread	Prawns
Mini samosa	Mini vegetable spring rolls
Piece of Stilton cheese	Small slice pizza
Breaded chicken piece	Few crisps
Sour cream dip	Cheese & pineapple

Approx. Calories   650   **1750**

At buffets, always go to the table once, make your choices, fill your plate and never go back! If you pick at the buffet, or make return journeys, your resolve will weaken and you will lose track of how much you have had.